THE RISE OF
TYRANNY

THE RISE OF
TYRANNY

JONATHAN W. EMORD

SENTINEL PRESS
WASHINGTON, D.C.

THE RISE OF TYRANNY
Copyright © 2008 by Jonathan W. Emord. All rights reserved. No part of this publication may be used or reproduced in any manner whatsoever without written permission except in the case of brief quotations embodied in critical articles or reviews.

First published in 2008 by SENTINEL PRESS, 1050 Seventeenth Street, NW, Washington, D.C. 20036

Sentinel Press
1050 Seventeenth Street, N.W.
Suite 600
Washington, D.C. 20036
(202) 466-6937

ISBN-13: 978-0-9820595-0-0
ISBN-10: 0-9820595-0-7

Library of Congress Control Number: 2008935384
Emord, Jonathan, 1961—
    The Rise of Tyranny / by Jonathan W. Emord
        p. cm.
    Includes bibliographical references and index
    ISBN 0-9820595-0-7 (alk. paper)
    1. Delegated legislation – United States. 2. Administrative procedure – United States. 3. Pharmaceutical industry – United States. 4. United States Congress – Power and duties. 5. United States – Constitutional law. I. Title.

Design by Suchavadee Ampaichitt

First edition: September 2008
10 9 8 7 6 5 4 3 2 1
Printed in the United States of America.

To my beloved son and daughter, Justice and Angelica Emord, that they may live to see the United States restore the founders' Constitution rededicated to its only legitimate, and paramount, end: the defense of the people's liberties.

The preservation of the sacred fire of liberty, and the destiny of the republican model of government, are justly considered deeply, perhaps as finally, staked on the experiment entrusted to the hands of the American people.

--George Washington

CONTENTS

Introduction   **1**
Prologue   **8**

1. The Founders' Commitment to Separation of Powers   **14**
2. Congressional Relinquishment of the Power to Make Laws   **21**
3. Industry Capture and Monopoly Rents   **29**
4. The Rise of Tyranny   **40**
5. FDA Approval of Unsafe Drugs   **47**
6. FDA Censorship of Health Information   **67**
7. FDA and DEA Destruction of Competition   **91**
8. CMS Elimination of Innovation in Medicine   **95**
9. The Way Back to Liberty   **102**

Epilogue   **119**
Notes   **122**
Index   **145**

INTRODUCTION

Little did I know when I wrote a paper on the framers' intent for my law school First Amendment seminar class that it would end up on the desk of the Commissioner of the Federal Communications Commission and land me a job as an attorney in the Mass Media Bureau of the FCC, an agency I thought then and still think now should not exist.

I had campaigned for Ronald Reagan while a student at the University of Illinois. Inspired by Reagan's call for a return to constitutional government through a roll-back of federal regulation and an elimination of several federal agencies, I founded an Americans for Reagan group on campus. Some twenty-five of us from an otherwise liberal university invaded the Midwest with campaign literature. I recall my political science professor telling me there was no way that Americans would elect a man as conservative as Ronald Reagan, and, yet, call it the naiveté of youth but I believed we could, and I also believed we could foment a revolution that would restore the founders' republic. On the first point, history proved me right. On the second, history proved me wrong. Indeed, our federal government has become a bureaucratic oligarchy scarcely resembling the limited federal republic the founders created.

In 1985, I received a call out of the blue from FCC Chairman Mark Fowler's Chief of Staff, Jerry Fritz. Fritz told me that Chairman Fowler had read and enjoyed my First Amendment seminar paper and wanted to know if I would work for the Federal Communications Commission. I remember posing the question, "how can I work for an agency that I do not believe should exist?" My concerns were allayed, however, by Fritz's explanation that the Fowler regime was serious about deregulation. I came to appreciate that Mark Fowler was one of those extremely rare agency heads, not heard of since, who would sacrifice his own skin, his own prospects for post-government employment, to eliminate as many unconstitutional and unnecessary regulations as possible. You see, he too was a true believer like the wise occupant of 1600 Pennsylvania Avenue who brought him there. His zeal, and that of his successor Dennis Patrick, to protect the Constitution and break down regulatory barriers to competition caused many communications industry leaders who benefited from the competitive barriers to despise Fowler and Patrick. Neither one was an industry lackey. Neither one could be intimidated by threats from industry that post-government employment prospects were dimmed by pro-competitive moves. Both were given two thumbs up from President Reagan who also chose to do what was constitutionally required rather than what was politically expedient. President Reagan never wavered in his stalwart defense of Fowler and Patrick, and they in turn never wavered in their commitment to the First Amendment and to free enterprise.

An idealistic lawyer of 24 years, I joined thousands of other young men and women intent on restoring constitutional government and free markets (we called ourselves Reaganites and Reagan Revolutionaries) who Reagan and his executive officers led into public service. Coming from towns across the United States, we were inspired by the Great Communicator (by his unshakable faith in the greatness of a free people) to use our youthful energies to take apart a bloated, anti-competitive, and unconstitutional bureaucracy.

Much was done to deregulate, but much more needed to be done when in 1988 the Great Communicator's second term ended. On Reagan's last day in office, I and many other Reaganites felt a profound sense of loss (and a foreboding sense of doom). We knew that Vice President George H. W. Bush could never hope to fill Reagan's shoes. Reagan was a giant in defense of the principles underlying the Constitution and a free market economy. His sincere belief in those principles and his affable manner, brilliant delivery, and poise gave him a stature many times greater than any other American pol, indeed a stature of near mythical proportions. He had become an icon who had moved the entire nation to respect the core values that underlay the founders' Constitution. When in his inaugural address, Reagan's hand picked successor, George H. W. Bush, pledged with ingratitude to build a "kinder and gentler" America (reading between the lines, "kinder and gentler" than America during the Reagan years), we knew the Reagan agenda was in serious trouble and would soon end.

We all knew there was no way that Bush could come close to replicating Reagan's greatness, but we came to realize that Bush had no intention of even attempting to maintain Reagan's deregulatory initiatives. Bush had none of Reagan's wit, humor, or intellectual honesty and had a like for bureaucracy that was the furthest thing from Reagan's sentiments. Bush never understood the libertarian heart of the Reagan Revolution and frankly thought those who did were mentally unstable. He preferred government as usual over government pared to its constitutional essentials; he had grown to love government through years of bureaucratic service, was in many respects the quintessential government bureaucrat even as President, and never quite understood why or how President Reagan managed to captivate the American people. The leadership qualities that were innate to Reagan, never came to Bush.

Bush senior thus reregulated. That ended the Reagan Revolution before it came to full fruition. Old guard moderates who favored the regulatory state filled the bureaucracy. The Reaganites left government for the private sector. The reregulation grew *pari passu* with new lobbying efforts aimed at exploiting the change in political climate. The old Washington game of obtaining from pro-industry regulatory heads anti-competitive regulations that protected market share had returned. The Clinton years were largely ones of autopilot because deregulatory initiatives were anemic and new regulatory initiatives, while unfortunate, were generally modest by comparison with George Bush junior's regime.

Another grotesque explosion in the size and scope of the regulatory state arrived when the younger Bush took office. George W. Bush achieved that end by combining an utter lack of presidential leadership and an ambivalence to deregulation with the appointment of many to executive positions in the bureaucracy who were dedicated to their own self-interest and that of industry at the expense of the American people. The result over the last eight years of Bush junior's administration has been an exponential growth in regulation and in government corruption combined with a massive new set of regulatory taxes, burdening most new market entrants to the benefit of large market incumbents. Although George W. Bush likened himself to President Reagan, he was unlike Reagan in every respect, having abandoned Reagan's ideology, having none of Reagan's eloquence, and having none of Reagan's natural affability and charm.

One industry, in particular, was given an enormous degree of political control over the United States government during Bush junior's years in office, the pharmaceutical industry. Although in my practice before the Food and Drug Administration I had come to know well that big pharma was the thousand pound guerilla always present when FDA made decisions, I did not appreciate just how extensive big pharma influenced the world outside the agency until I read Dr. John Abramson's eye-opening *Overdosed America* and interviewed him on my Health, Law and Politics radio program (www.talkstarradio.com). Abramson chronicles the pharmaceutical industry's creation of disease names and definitions, influence over medical school education, influence over physician prescription practices, and influence over professional publication along with big pharma's control of FDA and Congress. I did not appreciate how extensive big pharma dominated the agenda on Capitol Hill until I became educated by the staff of Congressman Ron Paul (and by the late Kent Snyder, the sage former Executive Director of The Liberty Committee), as I urged passage of the bill I wrote for the Congressman, the Health Freedom Protection Act.

Having practiced law in the nation's Capitol for over two decades, I have had direct interaction with key federal bureaucrats, members of Congress, and the courts. I now lay before the reader the terrible corruption and loss of principle that I have found along the way. I do so in the hope that those who cherish freedom will fight for a restoration of the constitutional republic the founders gave us. I pray for the day when our country may once again become, as Ronald Reagan was fond of saying, the last best hope on earth.[1]

---

[1] *See* Ronald Reagan, "A Time for Choosing" ("Rendezvous with Destiny"), Television Address on behalf of Senator Barry Goldwater, Republican Candidate for President of the United States, delivered October 27, 1964. President Reagan acquired the phrase from President Abraham Lincoln, who wrote these immortal lines one hundred years earlier on December 1, 1864 (from Lincoln's Annual Message to Congress):

This book is an exposé of sorts. It relates largely for the first time the history of industry's takeover of the government, using regulatory agencies and Congress as examples. I explain the foundations of liberty given to us by the founders and their prediction of our current state of peril. I do not hold back the truth, and I do what Congress refuses to do: identify precise steps to bring down the regulatory state and return the nation to its constitutional moorings and to a constitution of laws, not of men.[2] My hope is that Americans will resurrect the Constitution and remove from office those who use the instrumentalities of government to build private for-

---

Fellow-citizens, *we* cannot escape history. We of this Congress and this administration, will be remembered in spite of ourselves. No personal significance, or insignificance, can spare one or another of us. The fiery trial through which we pass, will light us down, in honor or dishonor, to the latest generation. We *say* we are for the Union. The world will not forget that we say this. We know how to save the Union. The world knows we do know how to save it. We -- even *we here* -- hold the power, and bear the responsibility. In *giving* freedom to the *slave*, we *assure* freedom to the *free* -- honorable alike in what we give, and what we preserve. We shall nobly save, or meanly lose, the last best hope of earth. Other means may succeed; this could not fail. The way is plain, peaceful, generous, just -- a way which, if followed, the world will forever applaud, and God must forever bless.

---

[2] From Article XXX, Massachusetts Constitution of 1780, quoted in 1 *The Founders' Constitution* (ed. by Philip B. Kurland and Ralph Lerner) (Liberty Fund, 1987) at 13-14: "In the government of this Commonwealth, the legislative department shall never exercise the executive and judicial powers, or either of them: The executive shall never exercise the legislative and judicial powers, or either of them: The judicial shall never exercise the legislative and executive powers, or either of them: to the end it may be *a government of laws and not of men.*" (emphasis added).

tunes and political fiefdoms at public expense. Our nation is too grand and majestic to suffer so lowly a fate.

PROLOGUE

Beginning in earnest in the 1930's, the United States Congress enacted legislation to create independent regulatory commissions and agencies. There are now over one hundred and eighty with annual budgets ranging from hundreds of millions to billions of dollars, including, but not limited to: the Bureau of Alcohol Tobacco and Firearms; the Centers for Medicare and Medicaid Services; the Commodity Futures Trading Commission; the Consumer Product Safety Commission; the Defense Advanced Research Projects Agency; the Drug Enforcement Administration; the Environmental Protection Agency; the Equal Employment Opportunity Commission; the Farm Credit Administration; the Federal Aviation Administration; the Federal Communications Commission; the Federal Election Commission; the Federal Emergency Management Agency; the Federal Energy Regulatory Commission; the Federal Highway Administration; the Federal Labor Relations Authority; the Federal Railroad Administration; the Federal Trade Commission; the Food and Drug Administration; the General Services Administration; the Internal Revenue Service; the International Trade Commission; the National Highway Traffic Safety Administration; the National Institutes of Health; the National Oceanic and Atmospheric Administration; the National Park Service; the National Telecommunications Information Administration; the Nuclear Regulatory Commission; the Office of Thrift Supervision; the Postal Regulatory Commission; the Securities and Exchange Commission; the Small Business Administration; the Social Security Administration; the U.S. Customs Service; the U.S. Fish and Wildlife Service; the U.S. Forest Service; and the U.S. Government Printing Office.

Collectively, the federal agencies and commissions regulate every important aspect of commerce in the United States. They are ruled by individuals who are appointed rather than elected.

The federal agencies and commissions have the power to create law through regulation without obtaining the consent of the people's elected representatives. They have the power to prosecute those whom they charge with violating their regulations. They often possess the power to judge the parties they prosecute without having to present the charges in the first instance to an independent and impartial court of law.

Throughout history that combination of powers (legislative, executive, and judicial) in single hands has been defined as tyrannical and despotic. Our founding fathers experienced tyranny of that sort firsthand, fought a revolution to relieve themselves of it, and created a Constitution that vests each of those powers in separate branches of government, replete with checks and balances to disable encroachments of power. They warned against collocation of those powers, reciting that if the collocation ever came to pass in this country, it would immediately spell the end of liberty and the rise of tyranny.

They called upon us to guard against that collocation of power. They informed us of the dangers of unbridled discretion, of power without balance, of the indissoluble links between aggregation of power and corruption and between governors' pursuit of self-interest and loss of human rights to life, liberty, and property.

In his *Notes on the State of Virginia* (1784), Thomas Jefferson understood well the tendency of governmental men, possessed of all three governing powers, to abuse those powers and violate the public trust in pursuit of self-interest:

> Mankind soon learn to make interested uses of every right and power which they possess, or may assume. The public money and public liberty, intended to have been deposited with three branches of magistracy, but found inadvertently to be in the hands of one only, will soon be discovered to be sources of wealth and dominion to those who hold them; distinguished, too, by this tempting circumstance, ...they are the instrument, as well as the object, of acquisition. With money we will get men, said Caesar, and with men we will get money. Nor should our assembly be deluded by the integrity of their own purposes, and conclude that these unlimited powers will never be abused, because [they] themselves are not disposed to abuse them. They should look forward to a time, and that not a distant one, when corruption in this, as in the country from which we derive our origin, will have seized the heads of government, and be spread by them through the body of the people; when they will purchase the voices of the people, and make them pay the price. . . . The time to guard against corruption and tyranny is before they shall have gotten hold on us. It is better to keep the wolf out of the fold, than to trust to drawing his teeth and talons after he shall have entered.

Our most sacred institutional principles (the union of which forms our palladium of liberty) have been trodden underfoot by agency and commission heads who have proceeded apace to use the instruments of government to enhance their own positions of influence and wealth. The consequences have been profoundly destructive for the republic. The republic our Constitution defines has been abandoned in favor of a bureaucratic oligarchy nowhere referenced in the document and decidedly against the core principles of the founders.

We have witnessed federal agencies and commissions on innumerable occasions take actions that would be soundly rejected by the voting public if only the public had a say in the matter, from the erection of barriers to market entry in every field of endeavor (that protect large, favored regulatees from new competition) to the approval of drugs so dangerous that they cause disabling injury and death to tens of thousands. The nation's resources have been pillaged by elected representatives and appointed officials. Our nation's leaders have sacrificed the rule of law, and the Constitution itself, in a headlong rush to build their own reserves of wealth and power. They have replaced liberty with tyranny and have caused the nation, as a whole, to lose its way.

From revolutionary America through the new nation period, the founders were unanimous in their belief that a combination of executive, legislative, and judicial powers in single hands would destroy liberty. Indeed, James Madison described the Constitution's separation of powers to be founded on a political truth of unparalleled significance. "No political truth is certainly of greater intrinsic value," he wrote, "or is stamped with the authority of more enlightened patrons of liberty" than the principle of separation of powers.[1] Like his founding brothers, Madison understood that "[t]he accumulation of all powers, legislative, executive, and judicial, in the same hands, whether of one, few, or many, and whether hereditary, self-appointed or elected, may justly be pronounced the very definition of tyranny." Jefferson likewise wrote in his *Notes on the State of Virginia* (1784) that the concentration of the three powers "in the same hands is precisely the definition of despotic government."[2] He explained that the Constitution in this respect depended on faith in the legislature to restrain its own power, because there was "no barrier" to prevent the Congress from encroaching on legislative or judicial powers. He said that while his Eighteenth Century contemporaries in the legislature might be "upright" in their adherence to constitutional limits on power, it would "not be a very long time" before legislative assumption of executive and judicial powers would take place.[3]

We now live in a country where three-quarters of all laws promulgated by the federal government are the product not of our elected representatives but of unelected officials, oligarchs, appointed to rule the administrative agencies and commissions, possessed of combined legislative, executive, and judicial powers. The institutions they govern were created by Congress over the last one hundred years. The Constitutional republic given us by the founding fathers no longer resembles its basic institutional design. The United States is now principally ruled by a centralized bureaucratic oligarchy, an oligarchy possessed of nearly unlimited powers. Agencies and commissions take action with virtually no check from the American people, the Congress, the Executive, or the Courts. The federal agencies are all powerful, outlive Presidents and members of Congress, and are largely unaccountable for their actions. Those who run them are the true governors of America, more powerful in their respective spheres than the President, the Congress, and the courts. They have absolute power within the areas of their jurisdiction, not unlike English monarchs who ruled before the Magna Carta (1215).

This book reminds us of our legacy of liberty from which the government and its present leaders recoil. It reminds us of the founders' design and of their warnings that if we deviated from that design to centralize power in single hands we would soon see our liberties sacrificed in favor of tyranny. It explains how our departure from the framers' design has in fact produced a pervasive tyranny, one that has caused a substantial loss of liberty, property, and even life. Select individuals and corporations have been destroyed or burdened to near destruction by actions of the federal regulatory agencies. The cost of regulatory enforcement upon the private sector must be in the tens of billions of dollars annually. That cost takes from the market resources that would otherwise help create jobs, sustain and expand industry, reduce prices, and fuel innovation capable of improving our standard of living and securing our competitive place in the world.

This book calls for a return to the founders' Constitution and its defense of liberty. It calls on us to vote out of office those responsible for the delegation of power that is destroying our republic. It offers a legislative agenda that could if implemented do much to restore the original Constitution with its system of separation of powers and checks and balances. It seeks a change in the standard for judicial review of administrative agency actions to bring about effective federal judicial review to help stop agency ruination of free enterprise. Only through measures such as those advocated here that revivify first principles and return the nation to its constitutional moorings will the American people enjoy prosperity and the full blessings of liberty.

1

THE FOUNDERS' COMMITMENT TO SEPARATION OF POWERS

The Founding Fathers greatly admired the Eighteenth Century French Enlightenment Philosopher Charles de Secondat de Montesquieu. They adopted Montesquieu's view that political liberty results from the separation of powers and incorporated that principle into the Constitution of the United States.[4]

In Federalist No. 47, James Madison revealed the wide acceptance among the founders of Montesquieu's call for separation of powers, describing Montesquieu as "the oracle . . . always consulted and cited on [the subject]."[5] In its effort in 1774 to convince the inhabitants of Quebec to support opposition to the Crown, the Continental Congress reminded the Canadians of "the immortal Montesquieu" and his association of liberty with separation of powers.[6] In instructing their representatives in Congress in 1776, the inhabitants of Boston declared it "essential to liberty, that the legislative, judicial, and executive powers of government be, as nearly as possible, independent, and separate from each other; for where they are united in the same persons, or number of persons, there would be wanting that mutual check which is the principal security against the making of arbitrary laws . . ."[7] They thus echoed Montesquieu.

In *Spirit of the Laws* (1748), Montesquieu warned against collocation in single hands of any two of the three legislative, executive, and judicial powers. He explained that the union of those powers would produce tyranny:

> When a legislative power is united with executive power in a single person or in a single body of the magistracy, there is no liberty, because one can fear that the same monarch or senate that makes tyrannical laws will execute them tyrannically.
>
> Nor is there liberty if the power of judging is not separate from legislative power and from executive power. If it were joined to legislative power, the power over the life and liberty of the citizens would be arbitrary, for the judge would be the legislator. If it were joined to executive power, the judge could have the force of an oppressor.
>
> All would be lost if the same man or the same body of principal men, either of nobles, or of the people, exercised these three powers: that of making the laws, that of executing public resolutions, and that of judging the crimes or the disputes of individuals.[8]

George Washington in his Farewell Address (1796); John Adams in his Thoughts on Government (1777); Sam Adams in his Declaration of Rights for the Commonwealth of Massachusetts (1774); James Madison in Federalist Nos. 47, 48, and 51; Alexander Hamilton in Federalist No. 71; and Thomas Jefferson in his *Notes on the State of Virginia* (Query 13) (1784) and in his Kentucky Resolutions (1798), each concurred with Montesquieu and warned against the collocation of the three powers legislative, executive, and judicial (or any two of them), recognizing that such concentration would lead to tyranny. John Adams wrote:

> I think a people cannot be long free, nor ever happy, whose government is in one assembly . . . [b]ecause a single assembly possessed of all the powers of government would make arbitrary laws for their own interest, execute all laws arbitrarily for their own interest, and adjudge all controversies in their own favor.[9]

Thomas Jefferson anticipated that at some future date the government of the United States would devolve into tyranny by committing legislative, executive, and judicial powers into single hands, recognizing that tendency to be an historic, recurrent pattern that would bring with it abuse and corruption.[10] Like Jefferson, Madison believed that without an eternally vigilant commitment to preserve the separation of, and limits on, power, the Constitution could not be counted upon as a defense but would become a mere "parchment barrier." He wrote: "[A] mere demarcation on parchment of the constitutional limits of the several departments is not a sufficient guard against those encroachments which lead to a tyrannical concentration of all the powers of government in the same hands."[11]

The founders believed political power, when concentrated in single hands, an immediate prelude to abuse and corruption. They agreed with Montesquieu who wrote: "[I]t has been eternally observed that any man who has power is led to abuse it; he continues until he finds limits."[12] In Federalist No. 48, Madison agreed: "It will not be denied, that power is of an encroaching nature, and that it ought to be effectually restrained from passing the limits assigned to it."[13] Those limits not only pertain to encroachments of power achieved when one branch of government presumes to exercise power that has been delegated to another but also when one branch of government presumes to delegate the powers vested in it to an entity outside of the Constitution's three branches.

The opposition political movement to the Hanoverian Kings made distrust of power a common theme, one adopted and admired by Whig revolutionaries on both sides of the Atlantic. Foremost among the Eighteenth Century popularizers of Whig thinking in England were Thomas Gordon and John Trenchard whose 144 letters on liberty, penned under the pseudonym Cato and published in the *London Journal* from 1720 to 1723, were variously known in the colonies and praised by the founders.[14] In 1774 James Burgh in his *Political Disquisitions* quoted with approval the following from Thomas Gordon: "men will never think they have enough, whilst they can take more; nor be content with a part, when they can seize the whole."[15] In his letter of February 2, 1816 to Joseph C. Cabell, Thomas Jefferson emphasized that ". . . the way to have good and safe government is not to trust it all to one but to divide it among the many . . ."[16] In his letter to Thomas Jefferson of October 17, 1788, James Madison wrote, "Wherever the real power in a Government lies, there is the danger of oppression."[17] In his Kentucky Resolutions (1798), Jefferson insisted: "In questions of power, then, let no more be heard of confidence in man, but bind him down from mischief by the chains of the Constitution."[18]

The Constitution reflects the commitment of the founders to avoid concentrations of power and, in particular, the vesting of any two of the three governing powers in single hands. Indeed, the Constitution vests the governing powers in three separate branches (Article I, legislative; Article II, executive; and Article III, judicial) and affords each an effective check on the other (e.g., Article I, Section 7, affords the president the power to veto bills from Congress and affords Congress upon a two-thirds vote the power to override a presidential veto; Article III, Section 2, has been interpreted to give the federal judiciary the power of federal judicial review but, in cases of appellate jurisdiction, gives Congress the power to determine the nature and scope of that jurisdiction; while Article II makes the President Commander in Chief, Article I gives the Congress the power to declare war and control war funding). The founders thus not only created a separation of powers but also a system of checks and balances to disperse and limit power and to burden the process of law making and law execution in ways that would prevent unnecessary action and would permit the arrest of unlawful action.

Moreover, the founders rejected the notion that the governing powers they vested in each branch of the government could be delegated to institutions outside of the three branches. As Nicholas J. Szabo reminds us: "Two maxims of law current at the founding were *delegate potestas non potest delegari*—a delegated authority cannot be again delegated, and *delegatus non potest delegare*—a delegate or deputy cannot appoint another."[19] Looking back upon the very first years of the republic, George Washington wrote in his Farewell Address:

> The spirit of encroachment tends to consolidate the powers of all the departments in one, and thus to create, whatever the form of government, a real despotism. A just estimate of that love of power, and proneness to abuse it, which predominates in the human heart, is sufficient to satisfy us of the truth of this position. The necessity of reciprocal checks in the exercise of political power, by dividing and distributing it into different depositories, and constituting each the guardian of the public weal against invasions by the others, has been evinced by experiments ancient and modern; some of them in our country and under our own eyes. To preserve them must be as necessary as to institute them.[20]

The Constitution, thus, was meant to serve as a counterweight to the formation of a despotic government, just as the Bill of Rights was meant to provide a barrier against government exercise of power in ways that would transgress the peoples' liberties. Neither the Constitution nor the Bill of Rights today serves as a reliably effective counter either to despotic government or to violation of the peoples' liberties.

One would think the federal courts a repository of power that, under the doctrine of federal judicial review, could stop violation of the non-delegation and separation of powers doctrines that the Constitution begets. Since 1984 and the Supreme Court's decision in *Chevron U.S.A., Inc. v. Natural Resources Defense Council, Inc.*,[21] however, the federal courts have largely abandoned that role. In testimony before the Subcommittee on Commercial and Administrative Law of the House Committee on the Judiciary (September 12, 1996), Cato Institute scholar Jerry Taylor wisely described *Chevron* as the pinnacle in the Court's destruction of effective judicial review of agency action:

> [The] line of cases [rejecting the non-delegation doctrine] culminates in Chevron . . ., in which the Court showed extraordinary deference to administrative agencies' interpretations of their own authority. The Chevron case arose out of a dispute over the meaning of the term "source" in the 1977 amendments to the Clean Air Act. Initially, the Environmental Protection Agency under President Carter defined the term so that it applied to each source of emissions within any given factory. But under the Reagan administration, the EPA issued a more flexible rule that considered the plant as a whole to be the "source." Though the Court found it impossible to discern a legislative intent with regard to this issue, it upheld the EPA's decision, holding that when a statute is silent on a particular issue, Congress can be understood to have delegated the power to make the law to the agency. And, according to Justice Stevens's majority opinion, "Such legislative regulations are given controlling weight unless they are arbitrary, capricious, or manifestly contrary to the statute." Professor Cass Sunstein of the

University of Chicago School of Law suggests that the Chevron precedent, which allows agencies to determine the extent and nature of their own authority, ignores the wisdom embodied in the old adage about trusting foxes to guard henhouses.

Since the 1960's, Congress has passed legislation containing sweeping aspirational goals for the administrative agencies to translate into action. To comprehend the translation, one must visit the Federal Register. There in hundreds of thousands of pages regulations in intimate detail govern industry. Oftentimes the rules bear little resemblance to the statutes from whence they purportedly came. Many times the rules effect results opposite those desired by Congress. It is not at all uncommon for regulations to impose requirements that contradict directly the statutory mandate.

The many extraordinary statutory delegations that feed the agencies and commissions power give them broad jurisdiction and autonomous governance, precisely what the founders defined as the very definition of tyranny. The Supreme Court has found no delegations of power from Congress to the federal agencies unconstitutional since 1935,[22] holding each one permissible merely upon finding that Congress has articulated some "intelligible principle to which the person or body authorized to [act] is directed to conform,"[23] ignoring the founders' demand for separation of powers and non-delegation.

2

CONGRESSIONAL RELINQUISHMENT OF THE POWER TO MAKE LAWS

Since 1935 Congress has delegated the power to create laws affecting every area of popular concern to independent regulatory agencies and commissions. Congress has been particularly eager to transfer combined law making, executive, and judicial powers to agencies and commissions in areas rife with public controversy, where taking a stand is a losing political proposition (i.e., where it will offend a majority or significant minority of voters, jeopardize campaign contributions, and reduce the likelihood of re-election). The transfer of power is, to be sure, an abdication by Congress of its central constitutional duty: to make laws.

Congress was expected to make decisions even if difficult or controversial but making those decisions invites public criticism and diminishes re-election prospects. The politician's lust for permanent office and power has won out over constitutional sensibilities. The incumbent politician's desire for control over his or her political destiny has created an overwhelming incentive for the transfer to administrative agencies of broad jurisdiction and powers. In that way, Congress has avoided the need to account directly for unpopular actions, deflecting public outcry toward the agencies despite Congress's ultimate blame for having relinquished decision-making power to those agencies in the first place.

Through this deflection of constituent attention, Congress has afforded itself a duplicitous out that avoids public accountability. A member who in fact supports an agency action to which a constituent objects can nevertheless relay the constituent's letter to the agency head, or write a separate letter chastising the agency head, to appease the angry constituent. The letter is in fact largely worthless because it does not involve an exercise of legislative power. The chastisement (whether a simple relay of the constituent letter or a letter of inquiry or criticism from the member) is in reality an act of legerdemain, of subterfuge. The member and the agency head both appreciate that the typical letter, particularly when just a conveyance of the constituent complaint, will be received and ignored or responded to in an essentially unresponsive and innocuous fashion. The letter may disguise a reality known to the member and possibly the agency that in fact the member supports the agency head's actions, has voted for appropriations to do the very thing to which the constituent objects, or has communicated to the agency head in private support for the action. In almost every case, the member will do nothing with his or her legislative power to rectify the constituent's problem and instead deflects the constituent's attention by rerouting the concern to the agency, knowing that to be a futile move (or, on occasion when a letter reveals a constituent's violation of a rule, an invitation to agency prosecution of the constituent). David Schoenbrod aptly summarized the politics of mass delegation of legislative powers:

[D]elegation allows legislators to claim credit for the benefits which a regulatory statute promises yet escape the blame for the burdens it will impose, because they do not issue the laws needed to achieve those benefits. The public inevitably must suffer regulatory burdens to realize regulatory benefits, but the laws will come from an agency that legislators can then criticize for imposing excessive burdens on their constituents.[24]

Schoenbrod explains how delegation not only writes out of the Constitution the non-delegation doctrine but also eliminates Article I's essential safeguards for the people's liberties: elected officials' need to account for the laws that govern the people. Schoenbrod writes:

Eancting laws, even laws that present difficult issues of interpretation, forces legislators to take political responsibility for imposing regulatory costs and benefits. In contrast, delegation allows Congress to stay silent about what the agency will prohibit, so it severs the link between the legislator's vote and the law, upon which depend both democractic accountability and the safeguards of liberty provided by Article I.[25]

An influential voice in the ears of the founders, John Locke warned against delegation of legislative power, explaining that it would violate the social compact by which the people consent to be governed:

The legislative cannot transfer the power of making laws to any other hands, for it being but a delegated power from the people, they who have it cannot pass it over to others. The people alone can appoint the form of the commonwealth, which is by constituting the legislative, and appointing in whose hands that shall be. And when the people have said, "We will submit and be governed by laws made by such men, and in such forms," nobody else can say other men shall make laws for them; nor can they be bound by any laws but such as are enacted by those whom they have chosen and authorized to make laws for them.

We need only look back seventy years, to the administration of President Franklin Delano Roosevelt, for the nation's first major experiment in delegation. Roosevelt's New Deal promised by act of Congress a massive transfer from the constitutional branches of government (to newly created agencies) of the power to make laws, to execute laws, and to judge law violations. For example, the National Industrial Recovery Act of 1933 (NIRA) granted the NIRA power to enforce price fixing and production restrictions. So extensive were the powers given that they provoked an utterance from Italian Dictator Benito Mussolini: "Ecco un ditatore!" (i.e., "Behold a dictator!").[26]

When Roosevelt commenced his campaign to transfer power, he was at first stymied by a Supreme Court unwilling to countenance the broad delegations. On May 27, 1935, the Supreme Court issued three unanimous opinions that held delegations of legislative power essential to the New Deal recovery program unconstitutional. In *Louisville Bank v. Radford*[27]; *Humphrey's Executor v. United States*[28]; *Schechter Poultry Corp. v. United States*[29] (which invalidated the aforementioned NIRA price controls and production restrictions delegated to the President), *U.S. v. Butler*[30]; *Carter v. Carter Coal Co.*[31]; and *Morehead v. New York ex rel. Tipaldo*[32], the High Court upheld the nondelegation doctrine. In *Schechter*, the Court held that "Congress is not permitted to abdicate or to transfer to others the essential legislative functions with which it is . . . vested."[33]

On February 5, 1937, President Roosevelt responded to the Supreme Court's actions by sending Congress the Judiciary Reorganization Bill of 1937 drafted at Roosevelt's request by his Attorney General Homer Cummings. The bill would add one justice to the Supreme Court for each of seven members who then exceeded the age of 70 and six months. Roosevelt aimed to add six pro-New Deal justices to the court in place of the six justices[34] who voted against the constitutionality of his programs. Although the bill never became law, the threat of its passage may well have produced the effect Roosevelt desired. Justices Hughes and Roberts sided with Justices Brandeis, Stone, and Cardozo to create a 5-4 majority in favor of the New Deal programs, what the media of the day referred to as "the switch in time that saved nine."[35] Justice Van Devanter, who believed the New Deal programs unconstitutional, retired from the bench. In his second term, Roosevelt nominated five pro-New Deal justices. Each was confirmed by the Senate.

Before the switch in time, the Justices by votes of 9-0 (*Schechter Poultry Corp. v. United States*); 9-0 (*Humphrey's Executor v. U.S.*); 9-0 (*United States v. Butler*); 8-1 (*Panama Refining Co. v. Ryan*); 6-3 (*Carter v. Carter Coal Company*); and 5-4 (*Railroad Retirement Bd. v. Alton R. Co.*) struck down as unconstitutional legislative delegations of power and violations of liberty or property rights protected by the Fifth and Fourteenth Amendments. After the switch in time, the New Deal legislation was upheld by the Supreme Court. Professor Bernard Siegan summarized the substantive effect of the change in Fifth and Fourteenth Amendment jurisprudence in *Economic Liberties and the Constitution*:

> Under its former policy, the High Court examined federal and state laws dealing with social and economic matters, and (under either the Fifth or Fourteenth Amendment) declared many unconstitutional because they deprived a plaintiff of property or liberty with-

out due process of law. By comparison, the contemporary Court will uphold such legislation unless it violates certain specially protected liberties or is devoid of all rationality. Laws fixing prices, entry, and output, or otherwise restricting production and distribution of goods and services, which could not have passed constitutional muster under the prior standard, have little difficulty surviving under the contemporary Court's rulings.[36]

The change also became a death knell for the nondelegation doctrine. Since the switch in time, no delegation of congressional power to an administrative agency or commission, regardless of its extent, has been held unconstitutional. Once a bastion of constitutional jurisprudence, the nondelegation doctrine has become a part of what Judge Douglas H. Ginsburg of the U.S. Court of Appeals for the D.C. Circuit has referred to as "the Constitution-in-Exile," a body of constitutional provisions and doctrines that have been written out of the Constitution by a jurisprudence that consistently brings down barriers to unlimited government.[37] Judge Ginsburg explains:

> So for 60 years the nondelegation doctrine has existed only as part of the Constitution-in-exile, along with the doctrines of enumerated powers, unconstitutional conditions, and substantive due process, and their textual cousins, the Necessary and Proper, Contracts, Takings, and Commerce Clauses. The memory of these ancient exiles, banished for standing in opposition to unlimited government, is kept alive by a few scholars who labor on in the hope of a restoration, a second coming of the Constitution of liberty-even if perhaps not in their own lifetimes.

Within the span of 74 years, some one hundred and eighty federal regulatory agencies and commissions have come into existence with vast new powers to create law. They regulate everything from the air we first breathe when born to the drugs we last receive as we die.

In the 1960s, Congress again expanded the power of the agencies with one major piece of legislation after another. The trend proceeded apace in the 1970's and in the 1990's. In *Presidents and the Politics of Agency Design*, David E. Lewis records:

> The administrative state grew tremendously during the 1946-97 period in the United States. The expansion of the bureaucracy began in the 1930s owing to the New Deal and the World War II mobilization effort. . . . In total, Congress created 182 agencies. . . . The greatest administrative growth took place during the Truman administration and the administrations of President Johnson and President Nixon. . . . [T]he 80th Congress (1947-48) . . . created twenty-one agencies . . . . President Johnson's Great Society Program also increased the size of the bureaucracy, with sixteen new agencies created by the 89th Congress (1965-66). A surprising amount of growth also occurred during the Nixon administration. Twelve agencies were created between 1969 and 1970, and fifteen between 1973 and 1974. Among the more prominent are the National Highway Traffic Safety Administration, Amtrak, and the Consumer Product Safety Commission.[38]

Today there is no matter of any economic or political import that is not regulated by a federal agency or commission. There is also almost no such matter to which the Congress acts unilaterally, rather than by simply affording more power to act to agencies and commissions. The law-making power while vested in an elected Congress by the Constitution is in fact routinely exercised by the appointed heads of the regulatory agencies and commissions. Neither the Congress nor the courts impose an effective check. We have created the very union of legislative, executive, and judicial powers that the founders described as tyranny. We are experiencing that tyranny now but still tolerate it (much like the urban myth concerning the frog in the boiling pot who got to his fate unwittingly by becoming acclimated to incremental increases in temperature[39]).

3

INDUSTRY CAPTURE AND MONOPOLY RENTS

In their ground-breaking *The Calculus of Consent; Logical Foundations of Constitutional Democracy* (1962), Nobel laureate James M. Buchanan along with Gordon Tullock developed the "public choice" theory of economics. That theory, in part, explains the behavior of federal regulatory agency and commission heads by associating their public actions with pursuit of self-interest. When political decisions favor self-interest they often come at the expense of the public. The threat of self-interest to the public becomes acute when an agency head is possessed of independent governing power. Today's bureaucratic law maker, prosecutor, and judge wields those plenary powers with virtually no sanction after the fact for the abusive exercise of discretion. Because self-interested actions by agency heads are so common, they now take place under the thinnest public interest veneer. They may have devastating effects on disfavored parties but the economic impact is usually limited to one part of an industry at any one time, and the action usually comes with a heavy dose of agency propaganda that casts doubt on the character or integrity of the institutions adversely affected. The courts rarely intercede to protect the victim and generally accept unquestioningly the agency's characterization of the complaining party and the agency's rationale for action against that party.

The prospect for lucrative post-government positions in the regulated industry, or in the bar or lobbying firms that serve the regulated industry, has become a major incentive for agency heads to issue decisions that favor prominent industry regulatees, often at considerable public expense and at the effective disenfranchisement of smaller industry players. Executives in prominent regulated firms appreciate the fact that agency heads who leave the government will very likely consider them as lucrative employment prospects. They use that leverage, often through well-paid Washington lobbyists and lawyers, to induce agency decision-makers to promulgate regulations that erect barriers to competitive entry or that render unlawful means of production, promotion, or sale used by their competitors.

A branch of public choice theory that Nobel laureate George J. Stigler pioneered, entitled the economic theory of regulation, or industry capture, helps explain how private firms induce agencies to adopt regulations that alter the law in ways that benefit them financially.[40] Industry capture promotes market concentration which has the effect of raising prices for goods and services, stifling innovation, reducing economic opportunity, and limiting consumer choice.

As government exercises jurisdiction over a market, usually with the acquiescence of industry leaders, it invariably relies upon those same leaders to advise it. Within a political environment where the one receiving the advice also has the power to create law which can affect market outcomes, the advice often devolves into an express or implicit quid-pro-quo, engineered in large measure in nonpublic deliberations between industry leaders and agency heads.

The industry usually agrees to concede to the agency a limited degree of control over an aspect of the market, often with the understanding that future regulations imposed over that segment of the market will add costs that can be absorbed by large firms but will be difficult or impossible to afford for small firms.

In 1967 economist Gordon Tullock first identified the substantive aspects of what later came to be known as "rent-seeking" in his study of monopolies.[41] In 1974 economist Anne Krueger coined the term, which may be understood as the means by which a party can manipulate the market or the law to bring about what is effectively a non-consensual transfer of wealth, causing one party or a small group to experience financial gains at the expense of all others. Typically lawyers and lobbyists for industry leaders will urge agency heads to promulgate regulations (prior restraints) upon an entire industry (not just those engaged in the disfavored activities) ostensibly to improve safety or quality or to eliminate certain politically disfavored outcomes. The underlying motive for the industry is, however, not a public good but private gain. The regulations recommended usually impose significant costs on all market participants, creating barriers to entry and new costs of doing business that may be unaffordable for smaller firms, driving them from the market. The result is a reduction in competition that redounds to the benefit of large firms that may enjoy a new ability to raise prices or consolidate market share and reduce funding for advertising, promotion, and innovation. Over time, consumers watch as the competitive market gives way to a government sponsored oligopoloy or monopoly, leading to higher prices, lower quality, and fewer choices.

> [U]nlike profit-seeking, rent-seeking doesn't create wealth, it merely transfers it from one party to another. Whoever wins rents by using political means may be better off, but others, potential

competitors, [and] more importantly consumers, will be made decidedly worse off. The latter will pay higher prices, get poorer quality, or have fewer choices because political means are quite effective in discouraging rival entrepreneurs. The results of rent-seeking also stifle the competitive discovery process, so that consumers are less likely to become aware of more efficient methods or better providers.[42]

Perhaps the best example of industry capture and rent seeking arises in the pharmaceutical industry. The pharmaceutical industry enjoys monopoly status through the FDA drug approval process and through long-lived patents. FDA's process restricts to single players the right to sell specific drugs. It does so through prior restraint on the right to market, the costly and politically sensitive FDA pre-market drug approval process. Pharmaceutical companies also enjoy statutorily extended patents that provide between 13.9 and 15.4 years of monopoly protection for their FDA-approved drugs.[43] Pharmaceutical companies also benefit from FDA enforcement against parties that make identical drug products but sell them illegally without FDA approval and against parties that make competitive therapeutic claims unlawfully without FDA approval. The regulatory costs of new drug approval are astronomical (over $860 million in 2004 dollars per drug[44]), thus limiting to a rarified few the right to participate in drug sales. The prior restraint on the right to make therapeutic claims is absolute, ensuring the pharmaceutical companies that their FDA-approved claims will experience no real competition.

Benefiting from monopoly protection from governments all over the world, the pharmaceutical industry has amassed great wealth (over $286 billion in U.S. prescription drug sales in 2007 alone[45]) and has invested part of that wealth in a sophisticated, comprehensive, and unceasing program of influence peddling, affecting:

(1) *education in the medical schools and among practitioners* (through lucrative pay packages and gifts to medical school faculty, teaching hospital staffs, and prominent scientists who write for medical journals and respond to media inquiries[46] and through an army of some 88,000 attractive sales representatives who visit physicians frequently and shower upon them free drug samples, gifts, and information promoting label and off-label use of drugs[47]);

(2) *medical research and the content of medical journals read by doctors, regulators and academics concerning the efficacy of drugs* (through medical research sponsorship and advertising sponsorship of those publications[48]);

(3) *prescription decisions of practitioners* (through valuable gifts for medical school students and practitioners who promote to patients specific drugs[49]);

(4) *regulations, policies, and decisions of the FDA Commissioner and the political heads of FDA Centers* (through the prospect of lucrative industry supported positions in drug companies; company or association sponsored chairs at universities and positions in law and lobbying firms); and

(5) *actions of members of Congress and the President* (through campaign contributions, gifts, lavish junkets, and industry supported positions after their public service ends).[50]

As Congressman Dan Burton (R-Ind) explains, the pharmaceutical industry has "unlimited resources" and "when they push real hard to get something accomplished in the Congress . . . they can get it."[51] The pharmaceutical industry's investment in rent-seeking includes extraordinary funding of the political war chests of incumbent members of Congress, regardless of party. In 2007, the pharmaceutical industry spent an estimated $168 million for lobbying the Congress of the United States. In the past decade, the industry's total lobbying expenditures exceed $1 billion.[52] The Center for Public Integrity finds that "more than 90 percent of the total" spent on lobbying by pharmaceutical interests in 2007 came from "40 companies and three trade groups: the Pharmaceutical Research and Manufacturers of America (PhRMA), the Biotechnology Industry Organization, and the Advanced Medical Technology Association."

The industry's success rate in blocking legislation against its interests and in securing passage of legislation in its favor is unparalleled. There is no other industry in the history of the United States, including the defense industry, that has enjoyed more largesse in the form of federal dollars transferred to them from the United States Treasury than the pharmaceutical industry. None has enjoyed more legal protection from competition than the pharmaceutical industry.

The passage of the Medicare Prescription Drug Improvement and Modernization Act (establishing Medicare Part D) reveals just how far the Congress will go to answer the call of the pharmaceutical industry. Second only to social security, the prescription drug bill is the largest welfare benefit in American history. It involves a massive transfer of wealth from taxpayers directly to the pharmaceutical industry. The bill went into effect with President George Bush's full endorsement.

The bill includes a remarkable provision that prohibits the federal government from using its purchasing power to negotiate reduced drug prices, something the U.S. Department of Veterans Affairs and the United States military have done for years. Consequently, under Medicare Part D taxpayers pay 58% more for drugs, on average, than the Veterans Administration, according to a study by Families USA.[53] Families USA found, for example, that a year's supply of 200 milligram Celebrex caplets under Medicare Part D is $946.44, compared to the Veterans Administration price of $632.09, and a year's supply of 20 milligram Zocor tablets under Medicare Part D is $1,485.96, compared to the Veterans Administration price of $127.44.[54] Families USA also found that Medicare pays 60% more than the Veterans Administration for the top 20 best-selling drugs.[55]

Because the drug industry is comprised of monopoly sellers of specific drugs, the prescription drug bill enables those monopolies to set the price the government must pay, in effect enabling the pharmaceutical industry to hold the nation hostage by depleting the U.S. Treasury at its will. The drug price no-negotiation provision was secured at the behest of the drug industry and the President by one of the Bush Administration's key point men in the House of Representatives, former Congressman Billy Tauzin, then Chairman of the House Energy and Commerce Committee. Tauzin steered the bill through the House, condoning much of the arm-twisting used to secure its passage.[56] In appreciation for his efforts, Tauzin was named the President and CEO of the Pharmaceutical Research and Manufacturers of America, the pharmaceutical industry's chief lobbying organization, with a generous salary of over $2.5 million per year.[57]

The annual cost of Medicare Part D is rising annually and is estimated to reach the staggering figure of $724 billion by 2015.[58] With the arrival of Medicare Part D, the country's already dire Social Security funding crisis grew exponentially into an insurmountable problem, leading former Comptroller General of the United States David M. Walker to sound an alarm in his January 2008 testimony before the Senate Committee on the Budget:

[T]he federal government's obligations for Medicare Part D alone exceed the unfunded obligations for Social Security. Health care spending systemwide continues to grow at an unsustainable pace . . . . . Medicare and Medicaid spending threaten to consume an untenable share of the budget and economy in the coming decades. The federal government has essentially written a "blank check" for these programs. . . . . In fact, if there is one thing that could bankrupt America, it's runaway health care costs.[59]

In 2007, veteran CBS News *60 Minutes* correspondent Steve Kroft exposed the influence peddling that led to the passage of the prescription drug bill, the costliest welfare measure in the last four decades. He interviewed two Congressmen concerning the influence exerted by the pharmaceutical industry over the Congress in securing passage of the prescription drug bill and in achieving insertion of the drug price no-negotiation provision. Kroft interviewed Congressman Walter Jones (R-N.C.). Jones told Kroft "[t]he pharmaceutical lobbyists wrote the bill." A massive 1,000 pages in length, the bill arrived at legislators' offices the morning before the 3AM vote on it, leaving little time for members to read its contents, let alone debate it. Another member interviewed by Kroft, Congressman Dan Burton (R-Ind), said that the vote on the bill came in the wee hours of the morning because those lobbying for the bill did not want the "shenanigans that were going on that night . . . on national television in primetime." Burton continued: "They're supposed to have 15 minutes to leave the voting machines open and [they were] open for almost three hours . . . The votes were there to defeat the bill for two hours and 45 minutes and we had leaders going around and gathering around individuals, trying to twist their arms to get them to change their votes." Jones described the evening as "the ugliest night I have ever seen in 22 years" in Congress.[60]

Among those lobbying for the bill were several former members of Congress on the pharma payroll, former Senators Dennis Deconcini (D-Ariz) and Steve Symms (R-Idaho) and former Congressmen Tom Downey (D-N.Y.); Vic Fazio (D-Calif.); Bill Paxon (R-N.Y.); and Robert Michel (R-Ill). When the bill passed, there were an estimated 1,000 pharmaceutical company lobbyists working it on the Hill. Congressman Jones told Kroft: "You couldn't even walk to the steps of the Capitol without having somebody, maybe one or two, coming up to you to say, 'Can't you change your vote? Can't you for this bill?'"[61]

Kroft reported that Congress was misled by the Administration on the price of the program, having been told falsely that it would cost no more than $395 billion over the first 10 years when in fact Medicare Chief Actuary Richard Foster conservatively estimated before the vote that the cost would be $534 billion. Congressman Burton said that many members who were informed of the actual estimate after the votes were cast said that they never would have voted for the bill had they known of the true estimate.

On March 19, 2004, Medicare Chief Actuary Foster testified before Congress that Thomas A. Scully, then Administrator of the Centers for Medicare and Medicaid Services, ordered him not to provide his cost estimate to Congress, stating that he, Scully, was "acting under direct White House orders." Foster testified that before the vote on the bill, he informed President Bush's special assistant for health policy, Doug Badger, and associate director of the White House Office of Management and Budget, James C. Capretta, of the estimate. Foster was specifically ordered not to respond to a pre-vote request for that information from the Chairman of the House Ways and Means Committee, Congressman Bill Thomas (R-Cal). Foster received an email from an aide to Scully warning Foster that he would experience "extremely severe" consequences if he provided the estimate to Congress.[62] At the very same time Scully ordered Foster not to provide his cost estimate to Congress, Scully conferred about post-government employment with law and lobbying firms, some of whom represented health care entities that stood to benefit from passage of the bill.[63]

Those responsible for ensuring passage of the prescription drug bill received lucrative jobs in the drug industry shortly after the bill became law. In addition to the $2.5 million annual salary landed by former Congressman Billy Tauzin from the Pharmaceutical Research and Manufacturers of America, other key players were rewarded by the industry. CBS's Kroft reported:

> John McManus, the staff director of the Ways and Means subcommittee on Health. Within a few months, he left Congress and started his own lobbying firm. Among his new clients were PhRMA, Pfizer, Eli Lilly and Merck.
>
> Linda Fishman, from the majority side of the Finance Committee, left to become a lobbyist with the drug manufacturer Amgen.
>
> Pat Morrisey, chief of staff of the Energy and Commerce Committee, took a job lobbying for drug companies Novartis and Hoffman-La Roche.
>
> Jeremy Allen went to Johnson and Johnson.
>
> Kathleen Weldon went to lobby for Biogen, a Bio-tech company.
>
> Jim Barnette left to lobby for Hoffman-La Roche.
>
> In all, at least 15 congressional staffers, congressmen and federal officials left to go to work for the pharmaceutical industry, whose profits were increased by several billion dollars.[64]

In a post-script to his story, Kroft explained that in January 2007 Democratic members of Congress endeavored to amend Medicare Part D to require negotiation of drug prices but the measure "was blocked in the Senate, due in part to the efforts of the drug lobby."[65]

The readily apparent pharmaceutical industry capture of the FDA and Congress is in macrocosm what occurs daily in microcosm at every federal agency and commission through the machinations of principal regulatees. Rent seeking through lobbied-for changes in regulations to protect the principal regulatees from competition by imposing substantial entry barriers and costs on new market entrants is the order of business for lawyers in the nation's Capitol. A veritable army of lobbyists whose primary mission it is to achieve rent seeking gains occupy hundreds of offices along the District of Columbia's famed K street and in other locations near the White House and the House and Senate office buildings.

4

THE RISE OF TYRANNY

The Food and Drug Administration, the Drug Enforcement Administration, and the Centers for Medicare and Medicaid Services are three paradigms of combined legislative, executive, and judicial powers that have devolved into cesspools of abuse and corruption. While study of other agencies would no doubt yield evidence of similar corruption, these three agencies are illustrative.

The FDA, DEA, and CMS have fulfilled the dire prediction of the founders that the union of the three governing powers in single hands would beget tyranny, as those in charge of the agencies use the instrumentalities of government to pursue their own self interest. Each of these agencies is ruled by one all powerful leader, an essential dictatorship. The FDA has one head in its Commissioner. The Commissioner of FDA can promulgate any rule, can overrule any judgment of agency medical reviewers, can order the prosecution of any regulatee, and can approve for marketing any drug, regardless of the scientific evidence that may exist against the drug's safety or efficacy.

The Congress of the United States has vested in one person the enormous power to regulate everything we consume and use for our sustenance and health—all food, drugs, cosmetics, biologics, medical devices, and dietary supplements. There is little real check on the exercise of the FDA Commissioner's discretion, not from the Courts, not from the Congress, and not from the President. The union of legislative and executive powers within FDA has yielded corruption, as the founders predicted, in the form of industry favoritism.

Likewise, the DEA has one all powerful head in its Administrator. The DEA Administrator can promulgate any rule or decision she desires, regardless of its economic impact. In her sphere of influence, she is all powerful. There is little real check on the exercise of the DEA Administrator's discretion, not from the Courts, not from the Congress, and not from the President. Here too, corruption exists in the form of industry favoritism.

The Administrator of the Centers for Medicare and Medicaid Services through Medicare contract carriers (insurance companies under contract to administer the payment of Medicare reimbursements to physicians) exercises vast control over the nature, quality, and quantity of medical care provided to almost every American aged 65 and older. Through that system, physicians accused of improperly billing Medicare are presumed guilty until proven innocent, are forced on pain of exorbitant interest penalties, withholding of tax refunds, and blacklisting on a national database, to pay the amounts in dispute long before a final and binding order, and are made to seek vindication in a five layered appellate review system virtually guaranteed to exhaust their resources in legal fees before they are ever permitted to seek vindication in a court of law.

In all three agencies, there are favored regulatees who have essentially come to affect or control political and legal outcomes. At the FDA, that favored regulatee is the pharmaceutical industry (and, more particularly, specific actors within that industry). At the

DEA, that favored regulatee is again the pharmaceutical industry, which now enjoys above market rates of return due to DEA enforcement to remove from the market independent suppliers of ephedrine and pseudoephedrine containing cough and cold remedies. At CMS, that favored regulatee is the insurance industry which, in turn, is a proxy for the pharmaceutical industry.

We can perceive abuses whenever agency actions sacrifice fundamental rights to life, liberty, and property to yield outcomes favorable to a preferred regulatee. At FDA, the agency's Commissioner has repeatedly approved drugs that the agency's own medical reviewers have deemed too unsafe to enter the market, thus favoring the pharmaceutical company proponent of the drug over the American public. The results have been catastrophic, leading to tens of thousands of deaths and injuries. Likewise, FDA maintains a pervasive censorship over therapeutic claims for foods and dietary supplements to ensure that the drug industry enjoys a federally enforced monopoly on the right to communicate treatment information. At DEA, the agency's Administrator has driven out of existence some 50 independent suppliers of cough and cold remedies, resulting in the loss of thousands of jobs, actions that financially benefit drug company suppliers to the traditional pharmacies. At CMS, the agency has permitted its contract carriers to audit and demand reimbursement of Medicare funds from practitioners who supply non-Medicare covered services, do not bill Medicare for those services, and are nonetheless denied Medicare reimbursement for the services Medicare does cover—all on the basis that the practitioners have provided non-Medicare covered and non-billed services that Medicare disfavors.

Many FDA whistleblowers have explained that within the agency political managers (those appointed by the Commissioner to head the agency centers and their underlings) have threatened them with retaliation for submitting intra-agency safety reports recommending against drug approval, or in favor of label warnings. Many have explained that they have been punished for testifying before Congress concerning FDA approval of unsafe drugs. FDA political managers have been accused of ostracizing scientists who oppose drug approvals, cutting them off from further safety review work and limiting their prospects for advancement in the agency. Some have described being treated as if they did not exist, with agency managers neither speaking to them nor responding to them, cut off from work and from associations within the work place. FDA Commissioners have been accused of using the agency's Office of Internal Affairs to interrogate and intimidate dissenting medical reviewers, forcing some to expend huge amounts in their own legal defense or to resign from the agency to avoid further abuse. The FDA Associate Director of the Office of Drug Safety, Dr. David J. Graham, stated that former FDA Commissioner Lester A. Crawford offered him a promotion to a position as an advisor to the Commissioner in exchange for not giving testimony on November 18, 2004, before the U.S. Senate Finance Committee, then chaired by Senator Charles Grassley (R-IA). Graham refused the offer.

On September 23, 2005, Crawford resigned as FDA Commissioner on the heals of a federal investigation into sworn statements he had made that he did not hold stock in companies that regularly did business before the FDA. In point of fact, Crawford did. Crawford pled guilty in 2006 to misdemeanor charges for hiding from authorities his ownership of that stock but copped a plea that avoided jail time. He resigned just two months after being confirmed as FDA Commissioner.[66] A key figure in the defense of the pain killer Vioxx before its unceremonious removal from the market for causing over one hundred and forty thousand heart attacks, including some sixty thousand deaths, Crawford was rewarded for his efforts with a lucrative position as Senior Counsel for the Washington lobbying firm Policy Directions, Inc., a firm that represents pharmaceutical companies, including Merck & Co., Inc., makers of Vioxx, and the Pharmaceutical Research and Manufacturers of America.[67]

In 2006, the Union of Concerned Scientists confidentially surveyed 997 FDA scientists. Sixty-one percent responded affirmatively to the question of whether they knew of cases in which HHS or FDA "political appointees [had] inappropriately injected themselves into FDA determinations or actions." One-fifth responded affirmatively to the question of whether they had "been asked, for non-scientific reasons, to inappropriately exclude or alter technical information or [their] scientific conclusions in a FDA scientific document." Less than half thought the FDA "routinely provides complete and accurate information to the public."[68]

The FDA Commissioner often relies on advisory panels consisting of scientists he or she selects to evaluate drug safety issues. The choice of whom to place on the panel oftentimes affects the outcome. That is particularly true when those with known conflicts of interest, with economic ties to the very company whose drug is being evaluated, are selected and the conflicts routinely waived. In 2006, the National Research Center for Women & Families evaluated FDA advisory committee meetings from January 1998 through December 2005. Based on its assessment, the NRC concluded:

> [M]any of today's FDA drug and device advisory committees are rubber stamps for approval almost every time they meet. Moreover, even when an overwhelming majority recommend "non-approval," there is a good chance that FDA officials will approve the product anyway. Approval is even more likely for medical devices than it is for drugs.[69]

In particular, NRC found that "when the FDA schedules meetings for several of its advisory committees, the outcome is almost certainly going to be FDA approval for the products under review." But when the advisory committees unexpectedly vote against drug approval, that does not detain the agency: "even lopsided votes against approval apparently do not have much weight, since the FDA subsequently approved many of those products." If a person were to think the advisory committees truly advisory, that would be a mistaken conclusion, according to the NRC: "Although FDA officials describe the advisory committees as providing diverse perspectives and expertise, the large number of unanimous or nearly unanimous votes suggests that either the data are exceptionally convincing or that the committee members are reluctant to disagree with their colleagues or believe that the FDA wants the advisory committee members to come to consensus." The committees are more political than scientific in that "many committee members' votes seem inconsistent with their concerns about the safety or efficacy of the drug or medical device under review" and "clearly illustrate the pressures that committee members describe to conform to their colleagues or to be able to vote 'yes' . . ."[70]

The Drug Enforcement Administration disenfranchises disfavored regulatees through revocation of the DEA registrations needed to sell, warehouse, and distribute scheduled listed chemicals. By regulation, DEA denies its administrative law judges who preside over registration revocation hearings the power to issue legally binding decisions. The decisions of the DEA's ALJs are advisory only, recommendations to the DEA Administrator who in fact issues the ultimate decision. The DEA Administrator, often acting through the DEA Deputy Administrator, is the one who brings the charges that form the basis for the revocation hearing. She is also the one who drafts the regulations that govern registrations. Consequently, the law-maker is also the prosecutor and the ultimate judge. There is no separation of functions. That method of decision-making has enabled the DEA Administrator to pursue a policy of routing out of the marketplace some 50 independent suppliers of cough and cold remedies to convenience stores, thereby protecting and expanding the major pharmaceutical companies market for those products in pharmacies (which are conspicuously left untouched by DEA). The pharmacies are serviced by the traditional pharmaceutical companies, for which DEA has a close and complimentary relationship.

The Centers for Medicare and Medicaid Services endeavor to force strict conformity to a one-size fits all approach that does not work in competent medical practice. Practitioners who innovate and rely upon integrative medicine (combining the best of conventional medicine with the latest scientific advancements in, e.g., nutrition therapy) find that their use of integrative medicine invites CMS contract carriers to audit them, deny them coverage for the very same services that Medicare covers in conventional practices, and force them into a long nightmare of CMS reimbursement demands, threats of prosecution, U.S. Treasury withholding of tax refunds, blacklisting on a national database, and a Kafkaesque labyrinth of legal appeals that seemingly go on forever, all designed to force through intimidation, coercion, and financial burden complete capitulation to CMS demands in every instance. The message sent to physicians is quite clear: One size fits all is the prescriptive remedy, even if it kills the patient.

5

FDA APPROVAL OF UNSAFE DRUGS

The Food and Drug Administration is a regulatory leviathan. FDA employs over 12,000 people and regulates products worth more than $1.5 trillion in annual sales. FDA thus regulates 10% of the entire U.S. economy.[71] Since the mid-1990s a steady stream of FDA scientists have fled the agency's Center for Drug Evaluation and Research when their consciences could no longer condone FDA approval of unsafe drugs. Without exception, each one has explained to Congress and the media that FDA is beholden to the drug industry, that FDA views the industry as its client, and that FDA does the industry's bidding by approving drugs as safe when the evidence reveals them to be unsafe (even to point of condoning death and serious injury). FDA's record is one of silencing scientific criticism, eliminating evidence of dissent, hiding critical reviews of drugs from the public, inviting industry leaders to participate in internal management of the agency's medical reviewers, and coordinating with industry leaders to use public resources to defend the reputations of regulated firms. Those forms of corruption recur in case after case with no substantive response from Congress or the President. To say that FDA's Commissioners have gotten away with murder is to speak literally.

Redux

In 1995 Dr. Leo Lutwak, the lead FDA medical reviewer for the diet drug Redux (dexfenfluramine, an appetite suppressant), objected to approval of the drug. "I, as the primary reviewer, felt the drug had low effectiveness and very high risk for neurotoxicity and pulmonary hypertension," Lutwak told the *Los Angeles Times*.[72] In particular, Lutwak was concerned that the drug would cause pulmonary hypertension, a rare and potentially fatal respiratory disorder. Lutwak was not alone in his objection to the drug. His immediate supervisor at FDA, Dr. Solomon Sobel, opposed market approval. Sobel told the *Times*, "I was supposed to sign off on that letter [i.e., the FDA letter approving the marketing of Redux] . . . . I told [an FDA manager, Dr. James] Bilstad that I would *not* sign on it. If he wanted to approve it, *he* should sign it. And the record shows, *he's* the one who signed it."[73] Indeed, Lutwak and Sobel's opposition to market approval mirrored the majority view of FDA's first advisory panel that assessed the drug's safety profile. The first panel voted 5 to 3 "that evidence of Redux's safety was 'not sufficient to warrant approval.'"[74] With the necessary acquiescence of then FDA Commissioner Jane E. Henney, Bilstad convened a second panel in November 1995. That second panel recommended market approval for the drug on a vote of 6 to 5.[75] Despite Lutwak's findings, FDA approved the drug. An estimated 18 million Americans consumed it.[76] On September 15, 1997, the drug was withdrawn from the market "after heart valve damage was detected in patients put on the drug." Indeed, "[c]ivil lawsuits . . . allege[d] that Redux caused the potentially fatal respiratory disorder that had worried Lutwak."[77] The drug was implicated in 123 deaths.[78] Wyeth-Ayerst Laboratories, maker of the drug, is a subsidiary of American Home Products. American Home Products ultimately paid approximately $4.83 billion to settle over 11,000 lawsuits involving the drug.[79]

Rezulin

In 1996 Lutwak (still at FDA) resurfaced as one of several agency medical reviewers who objected to FDA approval of the Warner-Lambert type-2 diabetes drug, Rezulin (troglitazone). FDA medical reviewer Dr. John L. Gueriguian was the first to sound the alarm about potentially serious liver and heart problems,[80] recommending in October of 1996 that FDA not approve the drug.[81] Gueriguian identified potential liver and heart toxicity.[82] In response, Dr. Murray M. Lumpkin, then Director of FDA's Center for Drug Evaluation and Research, ordered the removal of Gueriguian from the Rezulin review, a removal that was effectuated formally on November 4, 1996. As reported by the *Los Angeles Times*, Gueriguian's actual review of the drug was "purged . . . from agency files" before the drug was given "fast track" approval on January 29, 1997 by FDA management over staff objections.[83] In addition, Gueriguian's negative review was kept from the agency's drug advisory committee. The agency's political manager with oversight over Gueriguian, Dr. G. Alexander Fleming, kept Warner-Lambert executives abreast of the efforts of agency management to silence the FDA medical reviewers critical of the drug, as is evident from email correspondence unearthed by the *Los Angeles Times*:

> The FDA's banishment of Gueriguian clearly pleased Warner-Lambert's executive vice president for regulatory affairs, Irwin G. Martin, who e-mailed colleagues on Oct. 16, 1996, saying, "we're over the JG hurdle." Martin wrote that Fleming assured him,

"John [Geriguian] is 'out of the picture.' His review is complete . . . . It will not go to the advisory committee."[84]

So chummy were the FDA political managers and Warner-Lambert executives that Fleming sent the following email to Warner-Lambert's vice president Martin two days before the FDA advisory committee met, revealing foreknowledge of the likely outcome (something unremarkable because FDA political managers select the members of drug advisory committees): "The drug looks like it ought to be on the market. Loosen up and put on a good presentation. Call if you need help."[85] Then FDA Medical Officer Robert I. Misbin began to be concerned when he saw Gueriguian's predictions borne out in the market. Misbin had initially favored approval of the drug in January 1997,[86] then changed his mind after becoming increasingly convinced from adverse event reports sent to the agency that the incidence of liver failure was unacceptable.[87] FDA's Dr. David J. Graham made his objections public during the FDA advisory committee meeting on the drug in March 1996. Graham told the committee that Rezulin posed a threat of sudden liver failure for every user and that there existed no known medical means to protect patients from that occurrence. He further told the committee that with continued use came a greater risk of liver failure.[88] The committee did not heed Graham's warnings.

In December of 1997, finding the incidence of liver failure in the United States unacceptable, the British Medicines and Healthcare Products Regulatory Agency removed Rezulin from pharmacy shelves.[89]

Misbin wrote an email to his FDA superiors on January 24, 2000, stating "I see no reason why any well-informed physician would continue to prescribe [Rezulin]. Neither do I see any reason why FDA should delay in taking steps to remove [Rezulin] from the market."[90] If FDA did not remove the drug from the market, Misbin predicted "additional cases of preventable liver failure." In his Pulitzer prize winning exposé on FDA approval of unsafe drugs, *Los Angeles Times* reporter David Willman recorded the following observation from one of the scientists on the FDA advisory committee that approved Rezulin, Dr. Jules Hirsch, physician-in-chief emeritus at Rockefeller University in New York: "I'm really very concerned about the continued use of it. . . . I would not use it myself."[91]

Frustrated by FDA's refusal to remove the drug from the market and fearing that through inaction he would countenance deaths, Misbin wrote to a member of Congress pleading for legislative intervention to stop the marketing of the drug (stating in his letter, "I am writing to enlist your aid in convincing my superiors at FDA that Rezulin should be removed from the market because of its unacceptably high risk of causing liver failure"[92]).

The agency censored a scientific paper by Misbin that revealed the liver toxicity of Rezulin, denying him the right to publish it in a medical journal. "One of my supervisors said something to me that I have never forgotten," Misbin told reporter Michael Scherer, "that we have to maintain good relations with the drug companies because they are our customers."[93]

FDA aimed to silence its internal critics through intimidation. Lutwak, Gueriguian, and Misbin were all made subjects of a criminal investigation by FDA's Internal Affairs office. Lutwak explained to CBS that he was called before FDA Internal Affairs, accused of leaking documents to the media about the dangers of Rezulin, and when he denied having done that was told that if he "was lying" he would be "subject to criminal prosecution and five years imprisonment." Lutwak told CBS News Correspondent Sharyl Attkisson, "In my own agency I'm treated like . . . I'm treated worse than a criminal. I'm accused, I'm threatened, I'm taken away from my work."[94] Misbin was ordered to report to Internal Affairs, refused, and was disciplined.

Misbin, Lutwak, and Gueriguian all eventually resigned from the agency.[95] Rezulin was implicated in 391 deaths, including 63 from liver failure. The drug was removed from the market on March 22, 2000.[96] The *Los Angeles Times* quoted Dr. William L. Isley, an endocrinologist who helped develop Rezulin for Warner-Lambert, as saying: "The drug never should have gotten on the market. . . The whole thing is a travesty."[97]

Avandia

In April of 1999, FDA medical reviewer Robert I. Misbin reported to his FDA supervisors that a GlaxoSmithKline drug for type 2 diabetes then under review, Avandia (rosiglitazone), appeared to increase the incidence of congestive heart failure in study participants. In an April 2, 1999 internal FDA report on Avandia, Misbin warned: "My concern about deleterious long term effects on the heart should be addressed by requiring the Sponsor to provide adequate information in the label about changes in weight and lipids. A postmarketing study to address these issues needs to be a condition of approval."[98] His recommendation was rejected by agency managers.[99] On May 25, 1999, the FDA granted GlaxoSmithKline approval to market Avandia. In February 2006, another FDA medical reviewer, Dr. Rosemary Johann-Liang, advocated a black box warning to inform physicians and patients of the drugs risks to the heart.[100] Her recommendation was also ignored, and she was then subjected to managerial pressure.[101] Johann-Liang's supervisor, Dr. Mark Avigan, told her that agency management was "upset with [her] recommendation" and "decided to act like the review never happened."[102]

On May 21, 2007, the *New England Journal of Medicine* published a meta-analysis by Drs. Stephen Nissen and Kathy Wolski finding Avandia increased the risk of heart attack by 43%.[103] In

June of 2007, the House Energy and Commerce Subcommittee on Oversight and Investigations held hearings concerning Avandia. At those hearings, California Representative Diane E. Watson said that she had been taking Avandia for diabetes and developed a heart murmur from the drug. She told FDA Commissioner Andrew von Eschenbach, a witness before the Committee, "My doctor said, 'Get off of Avandia—there are other options out there.'" She criticized von Eschenbach for not including a heart attack warning on the Avandia label, stating, "you ought to have [the word] heart attack on the label, and I believe I was heading toward just that when I went to my physician."[104]

In June 2007, eight years after granting market approval to Avandia and a year and four months after Dr. Johann-Liang had called for a black box warning on the drug, FDA Commissioner von Eschenbach capitulated, announcing that black box warnings would be included on Avandia labels.[105]

In July of 2007 the FDA convened a drug advisory committee meeting at which FDA's Dr. David J. Graham spoke. Graham recommended that Avandia be removed from the market. Pressured to keep the product on the market despite the heart risks, the committee produced a schizophrenic result. The committee voted 20-3 that Avandia increases cardiac ischemic risk in type 2 diabetics but nonetheless voted in favor of keeping the drug on the market.[106]

Vioxx

FDA gave Merck & Co. approval to market Vioxx on May 20, 1999 without any labeling to warn physicians or consumers that the drug would increase heart attack risk. Prior to approving Vioxx, a study performed by Merck and submitted to the FDA revealed a seven-fold increase in the risk of heart attack from low dose Vioxx. A year after Merck received the go-ahead to market Vioxx, in November 2000, another Merck study revealed a five-fold increase in the risk of heart attack from high-dose Vioxx. FDA took no action based on that information.[107]

In August 2004, FDA's Dr. Graham told his supervisors that his research revealed high-dose prescriptions of Vioxx tripled the risk of heart attack.[108] The acting director of the Center for Drug Evaluation and Research, Dr. Steven K. Galson, denigrated Graham's evaluation, referring to it as "junk science." Galson also sent an email to the editor of *The Lancet*, a prestigious peer-reviewed British medical journal, calling into question Graham's "integrity."[109] Certain FDA managers began a general campaign to discredit Graham and control the negative publicity word of the heart attack risk was creating.

In early August of 2004, Dr. Graham presented to his FDA supervisors a large epidemiologic study he had performed on Vioxx with Kaiser Permanente in California. That study revealed that high-dose Vioxx significantly increased the risk of heart attacks and sudden death. Graham intended to present the data at the International Conference on Pharmacoepidemiology in Bordeaux, France. Graham recommended that the agency warn against prescription of high doses. In response, senior FDA officials ordered Graham to change his conclusions and recommendations and threatened that if he did not, he would not be permitted to present findings at the Bordeaux conference. An email from the Director of the Office of New Drugs explained that FDA was "not contemplating" a warning against use of high dose Vioxx and that Dr. Graham's conclusions should be changed.[110]

In mid-August of 2004, despite the evidence associating low and high dose Vioxx with significantly increased risks of heart attack, FDA announced that it approved the drug for use in children with rheumatoid arthritis.[111] The approval left several FDA medical reviewers incredulous: How on earth could FDA approve Vioxx for use in children in the presence of evidence that the product significantly increased the risk of heart attacks in adults?

On September 30, 2004, against a backdrop of mounting evidence concerning the lack of safety of Vioxx, Merck & Co. surprised FDA management with an about face, choosing that day to withdraw the drug from the market.[112] FDA and Merck communicated word of the withdrawal to hospitals and physicians' offices around the country. Drugs in transit from nurses stations to patients were seized just short of delivery. Only eight days earlier, senior FDA managers in the Office of Drug Safety rejected evidence of a lack of safety as "scientific rumor" and dogmatically insisted that Vioxx was safe.[113] Now with the withdrawal of Vioxx, FDA senior management were left embarrassed and fearful of the intra-agency scapegoating that would follow. (After scandals involving a public crisis of confidence in FDA, the FDA Commissioner ordinarily tries to assign blame to a convenient scapegoat within the agency.) They were thus left to ponder who among them would be required to accept blame to avoid an admission of malfeasance by the FDA Commissioner.

Graham now had leverage. He had reason to be believed by members of Congress. He had quite a few allies within FDA, albeit none in management. He became a whistleblower, contacting Senator Charles Grassley, then Chairman of the Senate Finance Committee, and relaying to him his evidence of FDA suppression of science, approval of unsafe drugs, and retaliation against agency medical reviewers who raised safety issues. In the wake of Merck's withdrawal of Vioxx from the market, Grassley ordered hearings on November 18, 2004 and invited Graham to testify.

Acting FDA Commissioner Lester A. Crawford did not want Graham to make public his findings about Vioxx and about agency foreknowledge of the heart attack risks. He also did not want public Graham's view of the culpability of FDA senior management for slavish acquiescence to industry demands, for censoring scientific dissent, and for retaliating against medical reviewers who raised safety objections. He feared Graham's views concerning the lack of safety of Bextra, SSRI antidepressants, Lotronex, and Rezulin would invite a general congressional inquiry into FDA's new drug approval process, revealing for the first time details long kept from public view through a combination of intimidation and character assassination.

When efforts by Graham's supervisors at intimidating him into not testifying before the Senate Finance Committee proved unsuccessful, new efforts were undertaken to disparage him with Senator Grassley's office and with others.

On the eve of Graham's Senate testimony, Commissioner Crawford tried once again to convince him that if he cooperated with management, he could secure a policy position in the Commissioner's office (along with a higher pay grade). As Graham relates, on October 9, 2004, a little over a week before his scheduled Senate testimony, "Dr. Crawford asked if I would come to the Commissioner's Office to oversee the revamping of drug safety at FDA. I explained that I was a scientist, not a manager or a bureaucrat, and I could think of 10 or 12 people outside of FDA who would be perfect for this job, especially if at the end of it, this person was told they could be the director of a new Center for Product Safety."[114] Dr. Graham further relates:

> The day before the Senate announced there would be a hearing at which I would be testifying, I was invited to the FDA commissioner's office where I was asked to consider leaving drug safety to move to the commissioner's office. This is very strange because over the two previous months, I had been vilified by FDA management in the press and attacked and harassed by my own management in an attempt to get me to change my conclusions about

Vioxx. Why would the commissioner want a vilified and hated "junk scientist" to move to his office to oversee revamping of drug safety at FDA? It just didn't make sense. And how did he know that I would be testifying? I imagine he was tipped off by senators friendly with industry.

After I turned down this offer, a series of "anonymous" phone calls were made by senior FDA managers to Senator Grassley's office . . . and to Tom Devine . . . These calls amounted to a smear campaign against me, maligning my character and integrity and accusing me of being a dishonest scientist and a liar. Some of these phone calls were made from government telephones (caller ID), which is a federal crime. Now the purpose of these calls was to discredit me as a witness and to possibly convince Senator Grassley that he should not have me testify, or if he did, then not to support or defend afterwards. With [Tom Devine and the Government Accountability Project], the purpose was to convince Tom that his group should not represent me.[115]

Despite the many efforts by FDA management to stop Dr. Graham from testifying, he testified nonetheless and did not hold back facts damaging to the agency. The information he conveyed was devastating. It sent shock waves through the agency, the regulated industry, the medical community, and the public. There testifying under oath was a twenty year veteran of the FDA, a senior medical scientist with the agency, announcing to the world that the agency for which he worked, that many erroneously believed protected the safety of their drugs, was "incapable of protecting America" and left the nation "virtually defenseless" against unsafe drugs.[116] That conclusion would have been shocking in and of itself but reasoned away by agency defenders were it not for the cold facts Dr. Graham conveyed in his testimony concerning what FDA knew, when it knew it, and how it let drug companies market to the world drugs that carried with them dangerous safety profiles. Indeed, at the time of its withdrawal from the market, Vioxx had become one of the most popularly prescribed anti-inflammatory and pain relieving medications in the world. Graham testified:

> Prior to approval of Vioxx, a study was performed by Merck named 090. This study found nearly a 7-fold increase in heart attack risk with low dose Vioxx. The labeling at approval said nothing about heart attack risks. In November 2000, another Merck clinical trial named VIGOR found a 5-fold increase in heart attack risk with high-dose Vioxx. The company said the drug was safe and that the comparison drug naproxen was protective. In 2002, a large epidemiologic study reported a 2-fold increase in heart attack risk with high-dose Vioxx and another study reported that naproxen did not affect heart attack risk. About 18 months after the VIGOR results were published, FDA made a labeling change about heart attack risk with high-dose Vioxx, but did not place this in the "Warnings" section. Also, it did not ban the high-dose formulation and its use. I believe such a ban should have been implemented. Of note, FDA's label change had absolutely no effect on how often high-dose Vioxx was prescribed, so what good did it achieve?
>
> In March of 2004, another epidemiologic study reported that both high-dose and low-dose Vioxx increased the risk of heart attacks compared to Vioxx's leading competitor, Celebrex. Our study, first reported in late August of this year, found that Vioxx increased the risk of heart attack and sudden death by 3.7 fold for high-dose and 1.5 fold for low-dose, compared to Celebrex. A study report describing this work was put on the FDA website on election day. Among many things, this report estimated that nearly 28,000 excess cases of heart attack or sudden cardiac death were caused by Vioxx. I emphasize to the Committee that this is an extremely conservative estimate. FDA always claims that random-

ized clinical trials provide the best data. If you apply the risk-levels seen in the 2 Merck trials, VIGOR and APPROVe, you obtain a more realistic and likely range of estimates for the number of excess cases in the U.S. This estimate ranges from 88,000 to 139,000 Americans. Of these, 30-40% probably died. For the survivors, their lives were changed forever. It's important to note that this range does not depend at all on the data from our Kaiser-FDA study. Indeed, Dr. Eric Topol . . . recently estimated up to 160,000 cases of heart attacks and strokes due to Vioxx, in an article published in the *New England Journal of Medicine*.[117]

After he testified, Graham obtained the legal assistance of Tom Devine of the nonprofit Government Accountability Project. The attempts of FDA managers to cause Devine to refrain from representing Graham, by calling into question Graham's credibility and reliability and labeling Graham's evaluations "junk science," failed.[118] Devine pressed for evidence of Graham's alleged ineptitude and nothing persuasive was forthcoming, thus failing to shake Devine's confidence in Graham.

Ketek

On February 13, 2007, FDA medical reviewer Dr. David B. Ross testified before the House Energy and Commerce Subcommittee on Oversight and Investigations. He testified that FDA had approved the antibiotic drug Ketek (telithromycin) "despite knowing that it could kill people from liver damage and that tens of millions of people would be exposed to it."[119] He explained that he "was called into my division director['s office] and told to 'soften my review.'"[120] He said that when he "made scientific arguments, they were ignored when there was an economic argument for the company."[121] FDA's lead medical officer for antimicrobial drug development and resistance initiatives, Dr. John Powers, joined Ross in opposing FDA's blanket market approval for the drug.

Ross testified that over his objection and that of others the agency knowingly permitted fraudulent data from a large Ketek safety study, identified as study 3014, to be presented at a January 2003 drug advisory committee meeting to determine whether the drug ought to be given market approval. The agency also failed to inform the committee of a criminal investigation then on-going concerning the false data.[122] The advisory committee recommended market approval for Ketek.[123] Ross writes:

> A routine FDA inspection of the practices of the physician who enrolled the most patients—more than 400—[in the Ketek drug safety study] uncovered fraud, including complete fabrication of patient enrollment. The inspector notified FDA criminal investigators, and the physician is currently serving a 57-month sentence in federal prison for her actions. Inspections of nine other sites enrolling high numbers of patients revealed serious violations of trial conduct, raising substantial concerns about the overall integrity of the study. In the end, 4 of the 10 inspected sites were referred for criminal investigation.
>
> Despite these discoveries, FDA managers presented study 3014 to the advisory committee in January 2003 without mentioning the issues of data integrity. The managers have stated that they were legally barred from disclosing the problems to the committee because there was an open criminal investigation, but they have not explained why the data were presented at all, in view of the evidence of the study's lack of integrity. Unaware of the integrity problems, the committee voted 11 to 1 to recommend approval of Ketek.[124]

Ketek was approved for marketing over Ross and Powers' objections in April of 2004 as an antibiotic treatment for bronchitis, sinusitis, and community-acquired pneumonia.[125] Ross found the political clout of Sanofi-Aventis the deciding factor for FDA, far more important than scientific integrity:

> Aventis got its drug approved. In my opinion, Aventis knowingly threw garbage data at the FDA and FDA let them get away with it. Why did FDA not investigate whether Aventis systematically covered up the problems? .... FDA apparently decided that if it's some small company that can't defend itself, then go ahead and make an example out of them, but not if it's the third-largest pharmaceutical company in the world. You don't want to get Sanofi-Aventis mad at you. FDA sent a terrible message that good conduct and bad conduct are going to be regarded as the same by FDA, at least if you have political clout.[126]

Ketek has been linked to dozens of cases of acute liver failure.[127] It remains on the market; over 6.1 million prescriptions of the drug have been issued.[128] Ross explains that even as late as June of 2006, after numerous cases of acute liver failure were linked to the drug, the FDA insisted on silencing internal criticism instead of acting to remove the drug from the market. "Industry has become FDA's client,"[129] Ross explained. "People at FDA know they have to be careful about not upsetting industry," he said.[130] Ross wrote:

> In the face of Congressional subpoenas and unfavorable publicity, reviewers at the FDA were warned at a June 2006 meeting by Andrew von Eschenbach, then the acting FDA commissioner, not to discuss Ketek outside the agency. By this time, 23 cases of acute severe liver injury and 12 cases of acute liver failure, 4 of them fatal, had been linked to Ketek. By the end of 2006, Ketek had been implicated in 53 cases of hepatotoxic effects. The FDA did not relabel Ketek to indicate its possible severe hepatotoxicity until 16 months after the first liver-failure cases became public. The with-

drawal of approval for two indications, acute bacterial sinusitis and acute exacerbation of chronic bronchitis, for which Ketek's efficacy had never been demonstrated, did not occur until February 12, 2007—only a day before the Congressional hearing on Ketek.[131]

Ross recalled one particularly horrific death caused by Ketek:

As it turned out, a number of people have died. The index case was a twenty-six-year-old man who took Ketek for an upper respiratory tract infection. He died a horrible death from acute liver failure, bleeding out of every orifice. He left behind two kids. How do you think his physician felt? He prescribed the drug based on FDA's approval.[132]

In February 12, 2007 testimony before the House Subcommittee on Oversight and Investigations, FDA's Dr. David J. Graham explained the Ketek blanket approval over FDA reviewers' objections, this way: "The FDA views industry as its client, and that's the only explanation here;" "FDA saw that it needed to align its interests with the company's, and the company's interest was 'get this drug approved.'"[133] "The Ketek story is about the FDA's betrayal of the public trust," Graham said. "Unfortunately, Ketek is not an anomaly."[134]

Paxil, Zoloft, and Effexor

In September 2003 FDA medical reviewer Dr. Andrew D. Mosholder discovered evidence that antidepressant drugs (serotonin reuptake inhibitors (SSRIs)), including Paxil, Zoloft, and Effexor, could increase the risk of suicidal thoughts in children.[135] FDA had assigned Mosholder the task of evaluating claims of an association between antidepressants and suicidal behavior in children in June of

2003.[136] Dr. Mosholder found evidence of increased risk of suicidal thoughts principally upon a review of twenty-two pediatric trials, involving 4,250 children.[137] He found "74 of the 2298 children taking antidepressants had a 'suicide related event' compared with 34 of the 1952 children taking placebos."[138] Over one hundred events occurred in the trials that were labeled by the drug company sponsors as "possibly suicide-related," ranging from hanging and overdose to cutting and slapping. Forty-seven patients were hospitalized; none completed a suicide attempt. Mosholder additionally found that only 3 in 15 pediatric depression trials included sufficient evidence of efficacy, raising the question of whether any of these drugs were effective in children.[139] He concluded, overall, that children in the studies who took antidepressants were on average twice as likely to have suicidal thoughts as those on placebo.[140] Mosholder's findings were leaked to the media. FDA Internal Affairs then began a criminal investigation of Mosholder.[141]

In the Summer of 2003 Britain's Medicines and Healthcare Products Regulatory Agency prohibited the prescription of the SSRI drug Paxil (sold in Britain under the name Seroxat) to depressed patients.[142] In December of 2003 the MHPRA declared antidepressants Zoloft, Lexapro, Celexa, Luvox, Serzone, Remeron, and Paxil unsuitable for those under eighteen years of age.[143] The Committee on Safety of Medicines, a subagency of the MHPRA, found "the risks of treating depressive illness in under 18s with certain SSRIs outweigh the benefits of treatment."[144]

Long before Mosholder issued his report, FDA management scheduled him to speak before a February 2, 2004 meeting of the FDA advisory committee considering safety risks associated with the prescription of SSRIs to children. Mosholder's negative findings caused FDA management to reconsider whether Mosholder should be allowed to speak. In January 2004, FDA's Director of the Division of Neuropharmacological Drug Products, Dr. Russell Katz, told Mosholder that he would not be permitted to present his findings to the committee. FDA's Dr. David J. Graham recalls the turn of events:

> [I]n early 2004, FDA suppressed another FDA scientist [referring to Mosholder] who had concluded that SSRI antidepressants increased the risk of suicidality in children. FDA held an advisory committee meeting where it hid this information from the public and from its own advisory committee. This suppression of important safety information was leaked to the press by people within FDA and this embarrassed the agency. My supervisor ordered an internal criminal investigation to identify and imprison the perpetrators.[145]

In a March 15, 2004 memo from Dr. Anne Trontell, Deputy Director of the Office of Drug Safety (the office in which Mosholder worked) to Division Director Katz, Trontell recommended that Katz permit wide dissemination of Mosholder's findings, stating that she and another Mosholder supervisor, Dr. Avigan, "share Dr. Mosholder's concern about the potential excess risk of self-injurious behavior in pediatric patients treated with SSRIs, and agree that these potential concerns should be transmitted widely to physicians, patients, and parents when these drugs are used." Agency management refused to give credence to Mosholder's findings, asking instead that drug sponsors supply more scientific evidence to support the drugs' safety in children and commissioning a new analysis of the data by Columbia University physicians. The Columbia University analysis, in the end, disappointed those who wanted to disprove the evidence of increased suicidality in juveniles because the report gave FDA managers nothing to conclude that Mosholder had been in error. The Columbia report largely mirrored Mosholder's conclusions.[146]

On September 14, 2004, FDA's advisory committee voted 18 to 5 to require manufacturers of antidepressants to include the following black box warning on those products:

> Antidepressants increased the risk of suicidal thinking and behavior (suicidality) in short-term studies in children and adolescents with Major Depressive Disorder (MDD) and other psychiatric disorders. Anyone considering the use of [Drug Name] or any other antidepressant in a child or adolescent must balance this risk with the clinical need. Patients who are started on therapy should be observed closely for clinical worsening, suicidality, or unusual changes in behavior.

Nonetheless, unlike in Britain, the FDA kept the SSRI antidepressants available for pediatric prescription.

The list of drugs above is but a small subset of the universe of drugs FDA has approved over safety objections from its own medical reviewers. Among others withdrawn from the market after FDA approved them as safe and effective: Omniflox, an antibiotic that caused hemolytic anemia; Trovan, an antibiotic that caused acute liver failure and death; Lotronex, a treatment for irritable bowel syndrome that caused ischemic colitis; Baycol, a cholesterol lowering drug that caused severe muscle injury, kidney failure and death; Bextra, a non-steroidal anti-inflammatory drug for arthritis and painful menstruation that caused heart attacks, strokes, and death; Seldane, an antihistamine that caused heart arrhythmias and death; and Propulsid, a drug for night-time heartburn that caused heart arrhythmias and death.[147] Before the Senate Finance Committee, Dr. David J. Graham, testified that other drugs still on the market were unsafe, including Accutane and Arava (for the treatment of rheumatoid arthritis) that cause "an unacceptably high risk of acute liver failure and death;"[148] Crestor (a cholesterol lowering drug) that causes myopathy and rhabdomyalysis; Meridia (a weight loss drug) that causes heart arrhythmias; and Serevent (an asthma drug) that causes a three-fold increase in the risk of death from asthma.[149]

Referring to FDA's history of silencing scientific dissent, Francesca Grifo, senior scientist and director of the Scientific Integrity Program at the Union of Concerned Scientists, stated: "Censoring scientists undermines our democracy and threatens public health. One stunning example: Vioxx. Fifty-five thousand Americans died because scientists at the Food and Drug Administration couldn't speak out."[150] According to FDA medical reviewer David Ross, "[e]ven if a product doesn't work or we don't know how it works, there is pressure on managers that gets transmitted down to reviewers to find some way of approving it. There's been a cultural shift at the FDA, and the pharmaceutical industry is now viewed as the client."[151] According to David Graham, "FDA is inherently biased in favor of the pharmaceutical industry. It views industry as its client, whose interests it must represent and advance. It views its primary mission as approving as many drugs as it can, regardless of whether the drugs are safe or needed."[152]

FDA's effective transfer of governing control to its primary regulatees is an act of corruption. FDA political appointees manipulate public resources for the aggrandizement and riches of pharmaceutical companies (and ultimately themselves) at the expense of American liberty, property, and life. They have betrayed the public trust and they have violated the Constitution they have sworn an oath to uphold. They have erected a tyrannical bureaucratic oligarchy that sacrifices the lives and property of the many to support the riches of a few.

6

FDA CENSORSHIP OF HEALTH INFORMATION

Thomas Jefferson in his Kentucky Resolutions (November 16, 1798 and December 3, 1799) and James Madison in his Virginia Resolutions (December 24, 1798) condemned the Alien and Sedition Acts of 1798, including their infamous prior restraint on seditious libel. They did so based on arguments that the First Amendment denied the federal government the power to abridge speech. The Alien and Sedition Acts did not survive the struggle, expiring in 1802 with the rise of the party of Jefferson, the Republicans. In all but one of its parts (the Alien Enemies Act still in force today), the Alien and Sedition Acts disappeared from the code books, but did Jefferson and Madison's views carry the day? One hundred and fourteen years later, in *Lee v. Weisman*, the Supreme Court finally recognized that the Alien and Sedition Acts undeniably violated the First Amendment,[153] but did that put an end to federal government use of prior restraints to censor speech?

Although some might suspect that with the expiry of the Alien and Sedition Acts and reaffirmation of the nation's commitment to the First Amendment, federal government prior restraints over speech would be banished (a relic of the Courts of Star Chamber in England and of the wicked regime of Henry VIII). They would need to think again, however. Since the 1930's, the Food and Drug Administration has maintained an absolute prior restraint on the communication of truthful nutrient-disease relationship information. The government has banished from the food and supplement marketplace scientific information contained in the peer-reviewed literature concerning how elements in foods (vitamins, minerals, amino acids, phytonutrients, enzymes, and other natural compounds) reduce the risk of, and treat, disease. From at least as early as the creation of the federal Food and Drug Administration on June 25, 1938 until enactment of the Nutrition Labeling and Education Act on November 8, 1990, the FDA has, with rare exceptions, prohibited every food and dietary supplement company from including on their product labels and in their product labeling any statement associating their products with the prevention or treatment of disease. Since 1990, it has continued to favor overwhelmingly the suppression of nutrition science over the disclosure of that science. In 1987, at the tail end of the Reagan administration, the FDA opened the door to allowing specific health claims on foods, but that door did not remain open for long. In the landmark decision of the United States Court of Appeals for the D.C. Circuit, *Pearson v. Shalala*,[154] the Court recited the relevant history this way:

> Prior to 1984, the FDA took the position that a statement that consumption of a *food* could prevent a particular disease was "tantamount to a claim that the food was a drug . . . and therefore that its sale was prohibited until a new drug application had been approved." H.R. REP. NO. 538, 101st Cong., 2d Sess. 9 (1990), *re-*

printed in 1990 U.S. CODE CONG. & ADMIN. NEWS 3336, 3338. But during the mid-1980s, companies began making health claims on foods without seeking new drug approval, a practice that the FDA supported in reglations proposed in 1987. *Id.* at 3338-39. Congress became concerned that health claims were increasingly common in the marketplace, and that the FDA had not issued clear, enforceable rules to regulate such claims. *Id.*

Against this background, and in light of the further concern that the FDA might lack statutory authority to permit health claims on foods without also requiring that the claim meet the premarket approval requirements applicable to drugs, *see id.*, Congress enacted the Nutrition Labeling and Education Act of 1990 (NLEA).

FDA's blanket prior restraint has suppressed an enormous volume of health information that could aid consumers in choosing which food and food elements to ingest to maximize their health by reducing disease risk and by retarding the progress of, mitigating, or curing disease.

The Food Drug and Cosmetic Act defines a drug based on its intended use, not its physiological effect on the body. Thus, under 21 U.S.C. § 321(g)(1)(B), a drug is defined as "articles *intended* for use in the diagnosis, cure, mitigation, treatment, or prevention of disease in man or other animals." Industry preference for this language has tremendous anti-competitive significance. To ensure control of the market for drugs, it is not enough to restrict to specific entities the right to sell certain substances. That is because others can claim that their different substances have the same or similar therapeutic effects. The drug industry must acquire control over the use of therapeutic speech in the market to exclude competition. If, for example, a party were able to claim that a substance treated disease without it being considered a "drug," then all of the Act's prohibitions on marketing a drug without FDA pre-market approval would be for naught. The industry could not be assured market protection and the utility of the Food Drug and Cosmetic Act to the drug industry would be at best very small indeed. Consequently, by defining a drug based on intended use, Congress gave FDA the sweeping jurisdiction over all ingestible substances that it needed to secure market protection for FDA approved pharmaceutical products.

The FDA regards evidence of an intent to sell a drug as proof that the product itself is a drug by virtue of the above statutory drug definition. Consequently, a food, like, for example, prune juice, if marketed with a statement that it treats chronic constipation becomes an unapproved new drug. An unapproved new drug can be seized and its sellers prosecuted and enjoined from selling the product. The drug definition enjoyed undiminished status for fifty-two years. In 1990, however, the drug definition experienced its first real competition, and neither the FDA nor the drug industry approved.

In response to overwhelming public demands for an end to zealous FDA efforts to remove dietary supplements from the market and to end censorship of nutrient-disease claims, in 1990 President Bush signed into law the Nutrition Labeling and Education Act. In particular, that Act included 21 U.S.C. § 343 (r)(3)(B)(i) concerning health claims (nutrient-disease relationship claims) for foods and 21 U.S.C. § (r)(5)(D) concerning health claims for dietary supplements. Under those provisions, anyone who wished to communicate a nutrient-disease relationship claim in connection with the sale of a food or dietary supplement could petition the FDA for pre-market approval and prove to FDA that the claim was backed by "significant scientific agreement." Proof of "significant scientific agreement" is defined in the statute as required for allowance of health claims on foods. Congress expressly gave FDA discretion in the statute to adopt another standard for dietary supplements, but FDA chose to rely on the food standard for supplements as well.

From the moment the health claims provision was conceived, the FDA and the drug industry viewed it as a means to undermine the new drug approval process and to challenge the drug industry's monopoly on the right to sell products for therapeutic purposes. In the rulemakings initiated to define the regulatory meaning of the new sections, FDA succeeded in virtually writing out of the law any way to make regular use of the provisions. FDA defined the standard for approval so high that it assured claim approval would be as rare as a finding of life on Mars.

In 1994, *New York Times* best selling authors, scientists, and devoted libertarians Durk Pearson and Sandy Shaw joined with a group of entities including the American Preventive Medical Association and Citizens for Health and directed me to file comments opposing FDA interpretation of the health claim standard for dietary supplements because it censored truthful information concerning the effect of certain nutrients on disease. In their comments Pearson and Shaw advocated that FDA adopt a bifurcated approach in which the agency would permit on the label and in labeling claims that were truthful (even if the claims were not backed by that level, degree, or quality of scientific evidence FDA deemed necessary to endorse a claim), leaving FDA with the option of including a disclaimer to make clear the agency's objections. In that way, consumers would not be deprived of emerging science indicating a potential disease risk reduction effect arising from a food element, and the FDA could state its view that the science was not sufficiently conclusive.

The agency under Commissioner David Kessler balked at Pearson and Shaw's disclaimer approach and insisted that claims be proven conclusively true, or near conclusively true, before FDA would allow them to reach consumers. Pearson and Shaw demanded that FDA permit four nutrient-disease relationship claims, for which Congress ordered FDA to receive comment, in light of an impressive amount of science supporting them. They asked that FDA permit a claim associating folic acid with a reduction in the risk of neural tube defect births, reciting the fact that every year Commissioner Kessler disallowed that claim he contributed to an estimated 2,500 preventable neural tube defect births, as 1 in approximately 1,000 pregnant women unaware of the need to consume 400 mcg or more of folic acid daily *before* they became pregnant experienced the horrific realization that their newborns would arrive with spina bifida or anencephaly.

Pearson and Shaw also asked that FDA permit a claim associating consumption of fiber with a reduction in the risk of colorectal cancer. They asked that FDA permit a claim associating consumption of antioxidant vitamins with a reduction in the risk of certain kinds of cancer, and they asked that FDA permit a claim associating consumption of omega-3 fatty acids with a reduction in the risk of coronary heart disease. FDA rejected all of the claims, despite the wealth of science supporting them, proving its intention to render the new health claims provision of the statute dead on arrival at the agency.

Many within the FDA sought to protect drugs from claim competition and to so ratchet up the standard for health claim approval as to make it virtually impossible to satisfy. In the first round, those forces won out (and, as we shall see, they remain defiantly in charge to this day).

Upon receipt of the FDA's decision not to define the standard for dietary supplement health claim approval in a way that would permit truthful speech to reach the market, Pearson and Shaw and other commenters directed me to sue the FDA. We filed suit in the United States District Court for the District of Columbia alleging violation of their First Amendment rights and explaining that the

FDA's censorship of the four claims condoned loss of life and needless suffering. We knew victory was a legal and moral imperative. We argued that FDA's failure to permit the disclaimer approach violated the First Amendment. We also argued that FDA's insistence on near conclusive proof as a condition precedent to permitting a claim caused truthful speech concerning inconclusive science to be unconstitutionally suppressed, and we argued that the agency's failure to define a standard discernable to the regulated class for claim approval violated the Fifth Amendment void for vagueness due process standard and the Administrative Procedure Act prohibition on arbitrary and capricious agency action.

At the District Court level, Pearson and Shaw lost.[155] The court deferred broadly to FDA, refusing to engage the First and Fifth Amendment issues. On appeal, however, Pearson and Shaw won in a landmark 3-0 decision in *Pearson v. Shalala*.[156] Never before had an entire regime of FDA content regulation been held unconstitutional under the First Amendment. Indeed, so confident was Department of Justice attorney Christine N. Kohl, who appeared on behalf of FDA, that she argued to the august appellate panel of Judges Laurence H. Silberman; Patricia M. Wald; and Merrick B. Garland that the First Amendment's strictures largely did not apply to FDA. Unpersuaded, Circuit Judge Silberman writing for a united court rejected the government's arguments seriatim. As to the first (that health claims lacking "significant scientific agreement" were inherently misleading and therefore not protected by the First Amendment), the Court dispatched the argument in this way:

> As best we understand the government, its first argument runs along the following lines: that health clams lacking "significant scientific agreement" are inherently misleading because they have such an awesome impact on consumers as to make it virtually impossible for them to exercise any judgment at *the point of sale*. It

would be as if the consumers were asked to buy something while hypnotized, and therefore they are bound to be misled. We think this contention is almost frivolous . . . We reject it.[157]

As to the second (that even if claims lacking "significant scientific agreement" are only *potentially* misleading, the government need not resort to disclaimers in lieu of outright suppression), the Court found the FDA's position directly contradicted by the Supreme Court's First Amendment precedent which favored disclosure of truthful information, stating, ". . . the [Supreme] Court has reaffirmed this principle, repeatedly pointing to disclaimers as constitutionally preferable to outright suppression."[158]

The court also agreed with Pearson and Shaw that FDA was obliged to explain what it meant by "significant scientific agreement" such that it would be "possible for the regulated class to perceive the principles which are guiding agency action." It therefore ordered FDA to "explain what it means by significant scientific agreement or, at minimum, what it does not mean."[159]

The FDA sought rehearing en banc from the full Court of Appeals, which effort failed in an 11-0 decision against FDA.[160] FDA then asked the Solicitor General to appeal the ruling to the Supreme Court, but the Solicitor General (who can decide such questions against the agency's request) rejected FDA's call for an appeal, letting the decision stand as final and binding.

One would think that a clear constitutional mandate of this kind would compel prompt corrective action. Not so. FDA ignored the decision for eighteen months and then issued new decisions condemning each of the claims the Court of Appeals ordered the agency to reconsider, doing so without evaluating, let alone accepting, disclaimers as less speech restrictive alternatives to outright suppression. FDA did not even revoke the four rules held unconstitutional by the Court of Appeals until October 3, 2000, eighteen months after the Court's decision, but simultaneously issued a new ruling banning all four claims in issue into the indefinite future.[161]

Those acts of renewed suppression in the face of the Court of Appeals' penultimate order that FDA accept disclosure over suppression led my clients to have me file a series of new law suits against the agency. In each, we argued that FDA violated the First Amendment mandate in *Pearson v. Shalala* and violated the Administrative Procedure Act's prohibition on arbitrary and capricious agency action and abuse of discretion. The District Court agreed, issuing injunctions against the agency and ordering FDA to come into compliance, but FDA would not.

In *Pearson v. Shalala II*, Durk Pearson and Sandy Shaw, Dr. Julian M. Whitaker, Pure Encapsulations, the American Preventive Medical Association, and XCEL Medical Pharmacy all sued FDA for its continued refusal to permit a folic acid-neural tube defect risk reduction claim for dietary supplements. That continued refusal the agency expressed in a letter to Jonathan Emord dated October 10, 2000. The claim had been among the ones reviewed by the Court of Appeals and found unconstitutionally suppressed but that constitutional mandate did not move FDA. The folic acid-neural tube defect claim had been proposed to FDA on January 28, 1994, and read: ".8 mg of folic acid in a dietary supplement is more effective in reducing the risk of neural tube defects than a lower amount in foods in common form." The scientific evidence documented that because of the volatile status of folate in plants (reduced significantly in storage, cutting, heating, and cooking of vegetables) and the superior bioavailability of folic acid in supplements, the only way for women of child-bearing age to obtain folic acid reliably in quantities needed for meaningful risk reduction was through dietary supplements, not through foods. Judge Gladys Kessler of the United States District Court for the District of Columbia found evidence of the superiority of supplement to plant sources well documented:

[C]ountless scientific bodies have expressed skepticism that food folate is as effective at reducing [neural tube defects] as is folic acid, including the Centers for Disease Control ("CDC"), the Food and Nutrition Board of the Institute of Medicine ("IOM"), and the national Center for Environmental Health ("NCEH") . . . The FDA does not seriously challenge any of these findings.[162]

The FDA refused to permit information concerning the superiority of supplement folic acid over food folate to reach the public, thus contributing to preventable neural tube defect births year after year. The District Court rejected FDA's position that supplement folic acid was not demonstrably superior to food folate, reasoning:

The question which must be answered under *Pearson* is whether there is any "credible evidence" that synthetic folic acid is superior to naturally occurring food folate . . . There clearly is such evidence, as the FDA itself acknowledged . . . (("IOM/NAS (1988) did note that the available evidence for a protective effect from folic acid is much stronger than that for food folate"). Consequently, the agency erred in concluding otherwise.[163]

The ban persisted from 1994 until 2001 (seven years, during which time women were needlessly deprived of the protective information in the market by FDA censorship). The harm to the public was palpable, consistent with the Court's findings:

[T]he public health risk from neural tube defects is undeniably substantial. [Neural tube defects (NTDs)] occur in approximately 1 of every 1,000 live births in the United States . . . Approximately 2,500 babies are born every year with an NTD. Of the children born with NTDs, most do not survive into adulthood, and those who do experience severe handicaps. The lifetime health costs associated with spina bifida, the most common NTD, exceed $500,000, and the yearly costs in Social Security payments exceed $82 million.[164]

Judge Gladys Kessler enjoined FDA's ban, holding it in violation of *Pearson v. Shalala I*. She recognized that FDA had abused its discretion:

> [T]he Court concludes that a preliminary injunction is warranted in this case. As will be explained below, it is clear that the FDA simply failed to comply with the constitutional guidelines outlined in *Pearson*. Indeed, the agency appears to have at best, misunderstood, and at worst, deliberately ignored, highly relevant portions of the Court of Appeals Opinion.
>
> * * * *
>
> In sum, the FDA has simply failed to adequately consider the teachings of *Pearson:* that the agency must shoulder a very heavy burden if it seeks to totally ban a particular health claim. With respect to the two disclaimers which the *Pearson* Court suggested might cure all potential misleadingness, the FDA did not consider one of them at all, and summarily rejected the other in a single sentence. Nor did the FDA "demonstrate with empirical evidence that disclaimers similar to the ones" suggested by the Court of Appeals would "bewilder consumers and fail to correct for deceptiveness." *Pearson*, 164 F.3d at 659-60. Indeed, the FDA did not consider *any* other disclaimers, except for, "The FDA has not evaluated this claim," a disclaimer no one has suggested and which is obviously inaccurate.
>
> For the reasons expressed above, the FDA's determination that the Folic Acid Claim is "inherently misleading" and cannot be cured by disclaimers is arbitrary and capricious, whether the two sub-

claims are examined in isolation or together. Consequently, the Court concludes that the FDA did not undertake the necessary analysis required by *Pearson*, especially as evidenced by its failure to consider clarifying disclaimers that could cure the alleged misleading nature of the Folic Acid Claim.

* * * *

Given that the scientific consensus, even as acknowledged by the FDA, confirms that taking folic acid substantially reduces a woman's risk of giving birth to an infant with a neural tube defect, the public interest is well served by permitting the information about the folic acid/NTD connection to reach as wide a public audience as possible. Plaintiffs' Folic Acid Claim, regardless of whether it is ideally worded or entirely free from misleadingness, communicates this vitally important message.[165]

One would think that having received a constitutional mandate from the Court of Appeals, and a strong rebuke from the District Court, FDA would finally favor disclosure over suppression, as the First Amendment and the Courts require. Not so. FDA responded to Judge Kessler's decision with more non-compliance and the filing of a motion for reconsideration. In *Pearson v. Shalala III*, Judge Kessler responded:

In moving for reconsideration, Defendants again seem to ignore the thrust of *Pearson I*. While that decision might leave certain specific issues to be fleshed out in the course of future litigation, the philosophy underlying *Pearson I* is perfectly clear: that the First Amendment analysis . . . applies in this case, and that if a health claim is not inherently misleading, the balance tilts in favor of disclaimers rather than suppression. In its motion for reconsideration, the FDA has again refused to accept the reality and finality of that conclusion by the Court of Appeals.[166]

Having been given a constitutional mandate by the Court of Appeals in *Pearson I,* having been rebuked in *Pearson II* and again in *Pearson III*, FDA nevertheless continued to suppress the very claims the Court of Appeals held unconstitutionally censored, refusing to favor disclosure over suppression. In a letter to Jonathan Emord dated February 9, 2001, FDA announced its decision not to allow a new, vitamin B6, B12, and Folic Acid-Vascular Disease claim. In a letter to Jonathan Emord dated May 4, 2001, FDA announced its decision to continue censoring the antioxidant vitamin-cancer risk reduction claim ("Consumption of antioxidant vitamins may reduce the risk of certain kinds of cancers"), which it had censored continuously since January 28, 1994.

My clients again directed me to file suit, proceeding against FDA's decisions in both cases. Once again FDA was taken to task for its noncompliance. In *Whitaker v. Thompson I*, Dr. Julian M. Whitaker, Pure Encapsulations, Wellness Lifestyles, Durk Pearson and Sandy Shaw, and the American Preventive Medical Association sued FDA for continuing to censor the antioxidant vitamin-cancer risk reduction claim. Judge Kessler used the opportunity to present FDA with a specific review standard. She ruled:

> *Pearson I* identified two situations in which a complete ban would be reasonable. First, when the "FDA has determined that *no* evidence supports [a health] claim," it may ban the claim completely. . . . Second, when the FDA determines that "evidence in support of the claim is qualitatively weaker than evidence against the claim— for example, where the claim rests on *only one or two old studies*, it may impose an outright ban. . . Even in these two situations, a complete ban would only be appropriate when
>
> > The government could demonstrate *with empirical evidence* that disclaimers similar to the ones [the Court]

suggested above ["the evidence in support of this claim is inconclusive" or "The FDA does not approve this claim"] would bewilder consumers and fail to correct for deceptiveness.[167]

Judge Kessler then assessed FDA's action against the above standard and found the standard not satisfied, determining instead that FDA had again disobeyed the Court of Appeals by favoring suppression over disclosure, contrary to the First Amendment mandate:

> First, while the Court of Appeals stated that a complete ban would be reasonable where there was *no* evidence to support a claim . . . that is not the case here. It is undisputed that the FDA identified *some* evidence (approximately one-third of the total evidence examined) in support of the Antioxidant Vitamin Claim. Therefore, a complete ban of the Claim cannot be justified.
>
> Second, the Court of Appeals stated that a claim might be banned if there was qualitatively weak supporting evidence found in "only one or two old studies." . . . The FDA has banned the Plaintiffs' claim by concluding that the evidence in support of it was weaker than evidence against it, but it is clear that *more than 60 recent studies* reviewed by the FDA supported the claim. This hardly constitutes the "one or two old studies" that the Court of Appeals contemplated might support a total ban.
>
> Third, even if the FDA's decision to ban the Claim could be justified by finding that the evidence in support of it was clearly qualitatively weaker than the evidence against it, the FDA has failed to provide empirical evidence that an appropriate disclaimer would confuse consumers and fail to correct for deceptiveness . . . Again, the FDA's decision to ban Plaintiffs' claim is not in accordance with *Pearson I*.

* * * *

Once again in its 2001 decision, the FDA has failed to recognize that its decision to suppress the Plaintiffs' Antioxidant Vitamin Claim does not comport with the First Amendment's clear preference for disclosure over suppression.[168]

In *Whitaker v. Thompson II*, the plaintiffs chose to up the ante against the agency. In light of the repeated instances of non-compliance with the Court of Appeals' decision, we made clear our intention to seek an order holding the FDA Commissioner and the Director of the Center for Food Safety and Applied Nutrition in contempt. To pursue a contempt action, we first needed an order directed specifically to those officers compelling them in their official capacity to abide by the Court's order. If then they did not, precedent would allow us to go after those government agents in their individual capacities, thus opening them directly to liability for the non-compliance. Early in the case, apparently sensing our direction, the agency chose to capitulate rather than defend against the action. On the eve of its filing of a motion opposing the Plaintiffs' motion for summary judgment, FDA permitted the B6, B12, Folic Acid-Vascular Disease claim ("As part of a well-balanced diet that is low in saturated fat and cholesterol, Folic Acid, Vitamin B6, and Vitamin B12 may reduce the risk of vascular disease") with a mutually agreeable disclaimer. The parties then filed a joint motion to dismiss the action. On April 2, 2001, Judge Friedman granted that motion.

Having been defeated in *Pearson I*, *Pearson II*, *Pearson III*, *Whitaker I*, and *Whitaker II*, FDA was still resolute in its unwillingness to make disclosure, rather than suppression, the order of the day. Instead, within the FDA Commissioner's and Chief Counsel's offices, the agency endeavored to create new rationales for supporting claim suppression.

One of those rationales, still in the works, concerns the development of empirical evidence to support the conclusion that consumers are hopelessly bewildered by nutrient-disease information and related disclaimers. The Court of Appeals in *Pearson I* did not rule out the possibility that in certain circumstances a claim may be incapable of being rendered nonmisleading through the use of disclaimers. The Court did state, however, that it was skeptical that such a happenstance would occur.

Another of those rationales, already implemented, involves redefining what constitutes a health claim. In 21 U.S.C. § 343(r)(1)(B), Congress defined any statement in labeling concerning the relationship of a nutrient "to a disease or a health-related condition" to be a health claim. Before the NLEA became law, FDA pressed upon Congress its desire that the statutory definition for "health claim" be the same as was contained in an FDA 1990 proposed rule (defining "health messages" as "the value that ingestion (e.g., reduced ingestion) of a dietary component may have in either lowering the risk, or forestalling the premature onset, of a particular chronic disease"[169]). Congress rejected that narrow definition, embracing instead the broad language that appears in the statute, making every claim that "characterizes the relationship of any nutrient . . . to a disease or health-related condition" one eligible for a health claim petition. FDA at first accepted Congress's broad definition in its implementing regulations.[170] In addition to the foregoing rejection of the narrow definition, Congress used the terms "disease treatment" and "disease prevention" interchangeably in referring to "health claims" in the House Report supporting passage of the NLEA.[171] Congress in its DSHEA Senate Report also made clear the congressional understanding that the term health claim embraced disease treatment claims.[172] The NLEA's health claim language, and the legislative intent underlying it, reveal that Congress did not intend to restrict the scope of health claims to instances in which nutrients lowered the risk of, or forestalled, disease but, rather, understood the language to embrace all relationships between nutrients and diseases, including those in which nutrients treat disease.

In *Whitaker v. Thompson III*, FDA's redefinition of the term health claim was put to the test. In a letter to Jonathan Emord dated December 1, 1999, FDA denied a claim from Dr. Julian M. Whitaker, Pure Encapsulations, Durk Pearson and Sandy Shaw, and the American Preventive Medical Association associating saw palmetto with a reduction in the symptoms of benign prostatic hypertrophe (a non-cancerous enlarged prostate) ("Consumption of 320 mg daily of Saw Palmetto extract may improve urine flow, reduce nocturia, and reduce voiding urgency associated with mild benign prostatic hyperplasia (BPH)"). It did so primarily on the basis that the claim concerned a nutrient's treatment effects on a disease. Without formal rulemaking and in an unexplained departure from its NLEA implementing regulations, FDA summarily revived its 1990 position that "health claims" refer only to disease risk lowering, or disease forestalling, claims. FDA took the position that only a drug could be accompanied with claims of disease treatment.

The plaintiffs filed suit on First Amendment and administrative law grounds, but this time the United States District Court deferred to FDA's reinterpretation of the rule under the *Chevron* doctrine and denied the plaintiffs relief.[173] On appeal, the United States Court of Appeals for the D.C. Circuit, Judge Stephen F. Williams writing for a panel that also included Judges Arthur Raymond Randolph and John Roberts (now a Supreme Court Justice), affirmed the District Court decision.[174] That affirmation, followed by the Supreme Court's denial of plaintiffs' petition for a writ of certiorari, gave FDA a legal predicate for unraveling the health claim regime. FDA moved quickly in that direction.

Although *Whitaker v. Thompson III* was not a resounding victory for FDA because it included grousing by the court concerning the statute's lack of clarity supportive of FDA's read, it was a victory nonetheless and sufficient to serve the agency's purposes. FDA now had precedent it could bend to undergird regulatory action that would censor truthful information concerning nutrient-disease relationships.

To that end, in several regulatory decisions following *Whitaker III*, FDA revealed that it considered scientific evidence evaluating the treatment effects of nutrients not germane to health claims, summarily excluding the evidence from consideration. In its significant scientific agreement guidance, the agency strongly suggested that only well-designed, large-scale, randomized, prospective, double-blind, placebo controlled clinical trials would suffice to support a claim. In its qualified health claim guidance, the agency likewise stated that it would provide less than draconian disclaimers only for those claims backed by clinical trials acceptable to the agency. By declaring treatment studies largely off limits, the FDA thus indicated that no qualified health claim would be given anything less than a draconian disclaimer. This, then, has achieved the goal of reducing health claims by discouraging their submission.

The FDA's exclusion of treatment studies is generally regarded by experts in nutrition as unscientific. Often treatment studies provide proof of a mechanism of action that supports a disease preventive effect. Consequently, treatment studies are usually germane to claims of prevention. Moreover, excluding that evidence from consideration tends to bias evaluations against claims.

Sooner or later FDA's discounting of treatment studies in its health claim reviews will be challenged in federal court. An enormous quantity of truthful information indispensable to the exercise of informed choice in the market will ride on the outcome of those struggles.

Another area that invites litigation involves FDA's persistent reduction in the scope of dietary supplement claims that are permitted without FDA approval, what the agency refers to as "structure/function claims." Structure/function claims are those that refer to an effect of a nutrient on a body structure or function without reference to disease. The Dietary Supplement Health and Education Act codified an exemption for structure/function claims from FDA prior approval.[175] FDA interprets whether a statement is a permitted structure/function claim or a prohibited drug claim based on its view of the statement's implied meaning. So, for example, a claim that a dietary supplement reduces cholesterol is undoubtedly one concerning the effect of a nutrient on a body structure or function but FDA holds to the view that cholesterol lowering is a drug function and, so, deems cholesterol lowering claims prohibited for dietary supplements even if (or especially if) true.

FDA exercises profound subjectivity in making these determinations. Often when a structure/function claim appears to trench on the interests of the drug industry, the agency condemns the claim as a prohibited drug claim. The truth of the claim is irrelevant to the determination, except to the extent that the drug industry ordinarily fears true structure/function claims that affect their markets more than false ones and, consequently, the FDA marches in lockstep.

Before *Whitaker v. Thompson III*, the drug industry relied upon proxies to do its bidding against supplement claims. It reserved the direct approach for confidential contacts with the political appointees in the Center for Drug Evaluation and Research, the Commissioner's office, and the Chief Counsel's office. In the health claims litigation, associations that receive funding from the drug industry have assumed central roles in opposing claims (and thereby supporting the drug industry's view), filing comments before the FDA and amicus pleadings in the federal courts.

When specific health claims have raised concern within the drug industry that dietary supplements may reduce drug market share, the FDA has been quick to suppress the claims. For example, in May 2003 the agency received a health claim petition seeking approval of claims associating glucosamine and chondroitin sulfate with a reduction in the risk of osteoarthritis. The evidence supporting the claims was substantial, as determined by independent scientific experts. If not censored by the agency, the claims would have informed the world that glucosamine and chondroitin sulfate were effective in rebuilding and repairing cartilage, thereby helping to reduce the risk and incidence of osteoarthritis. The most common form of arthritis, osteoarthritis afflicts 12% of the United States population age twenty-five and older (approximately 21 million people)).[176] Relief through the supplement could be achieved for a fraction of a cent a day.

The FDA's recommended (and commonly prescribed) treatments for osteoarthritis, the non-steroidal anti-inflammatory drugs (NSAIDs), reduce inflammation and mask pain but they do nothing to repair cartilage. Moreover, unlike glucosamine and chondroitin sulfate, they come with side-effects from long-term use (including, among others, kidney failure, liver failure, and ulcers). Consequently, people with osteoarthritis continue to experience degradation of their cartilage while on the NSAIDs, subtly deceived by the drug's anti-inflammatory and pain relieving properties. The ultimate effect of osteoarthritis is a debilitating erosion of cartilage resulting in painful bone on bone contact and friction, known as eburnation. Glucosamine and chondroitin sulfate help fend off eburnation by reconstructing and preserving existing cartilage that would otherwise be eliminated by advanced osteoarthritis.

At first, FDA seemed receptive to the glucosamine and chondroitin sulfate claims, indicating that at least some of them would be permitted; but then the Center for Drug Evaluation and

Research (CDER) weighed in, on behalf of its de facto client the makers of the NSAIDs. An FDA order was issued suppressing all of the claims. FDA management formed an expert advisory panel to review the science.

In all other instances, the FDA acted on health claim petitions following a review by the Center for Food Safety and Applied Nutrition without assignment of the claims to a Food Advisory panel. Not so with the glucosamine and chondroitin sulfate petition because of its concern to the NSAID makers. The agency wanted to hedge its bets anticipating an appeal.

Eleven of the seventeen experts FDA management selected for the panel had conflicts of interest in the form of direct and indirect financial ties to the NSAID industry. The heavily conflicted panel, steered carefully by FDA counsel and CDER representatives, predictably voted against claim allowance. After the decision, in a letter to me dated October 12, 2004, FDA Director of Regulatory Affairs Michael M. Landa simultaneously confessed the existence of the conflicts and then summarily dismissed their significance with these words:

> Conflicts of interest and waivers on the [Food Advisory Committee] are not unusual, because the world-renowned experts FDA seeks for its advisory committee are of course also much sought after by the private sector and by other government agencies. The law recognizes this tension and resolves it by providing for waivers; if a conflict of interest were sufficient to make a possible candidate for advisory committee membership ineligible for service without the possibility of a waiver, FDA would be unable to obtain the outside expertise it needs. Not surprisingly, then, FDA issued waivers to 11 of the other 17 members of the FAC.[177]

After *Whitaker v. Thompson III* the drug industry has become emboldened. *Whitaker v. Thompson III* invited a new approach to censorship of health information by confirming that FDA could lawfully censor all nutrient-disease treatment claims for dietary supplements, including truthful claims. The court thus invited FDA to define what constitutes a disease treatment (or drug) claim and to engage in a categorical suppression of those claims, regardless of their validity. Consequently, whenever FDA approves a new drug, it may now move to prohibit structure/function claims it previously allowed for dietary supplements on the basis that those terms have become biomarkers or symptoms of the newly defined disease and thus sucked into the drug vortex. If today overweight is considered a condition of health and not a disease, tomorrow FDA may proclaim it as a biomarker of or even a symptom of cancer, high blood pressure, or diabetes, removing it from the lexicon of allowable speech for dietary supplements. If today the production of free radicals may be considered a normal part of cell metabolism, tomorrow FDA may proclaim free radicals a biomarker of or even a symptom of cancer, cardiovascular disease, or cataracts, removing the term from the lexicon of allowable speech for dietary supplements. The wickedly viral extension of this rationale to almost every health effect of a nutrient on the body would render the structure/function claim exemption a dead letter and would carve out of the marketplace nearly all speech at the point of sale concerning nutrients' utility to consumers. This move would defeat the DSHEA and would create an effective *cordon sanitaire* (protective zone) around the pharmaceutical industry's monopoly on therapeutic claims.

Ordinarily shy about revealing any direct involvement in affecting supplement claim decisions at the agency (to preserve the false impression that FDA's drug center does not lord over the food center), at least one industry player has seen fit to demand a reclassification of claims in an overt manner, relying on *Whitaker III* for support. On April 17, 2008, drug giant GlaxoSmithKline submitted a petition to the FDA, joined by its compatriots the American Dietetic Association and the Obesity Society, among others. Glaxo asked FDA to ban all claims that a dietary supplement "promote[s], assist[s], or otherwise help[s] in weight loss." If overweight status is a contributing factor to a host of diseases, Glaxo argues, then claims concerning weight loss are drug claims that may be censored under *Whitaker III*.

Glaxo's bias and interest are apparent to industry observers, albeit undisclosed in the petition. The company achieved FDA approval for an over-the-counter weight loss drug called Alli (a lower dose version of the prescription drug Xenical (Orlistat)) that competes directly with weight loss supplements for market share. Unlike the supplements, however, Alli produces certain disagreeable, and potentially harmful, side effects including, by GlaxoSmithKline's own admission, diarrhea and reduced vitamin absorption.[178]

In its petition Glaxo asked FDA to prohibit all weight loss claims for dietary supplements and to do so summarily, without the benefit of rulemaking (that despite the fact that in 2000 FDA relied on rulemaking to conclude that weight loss claims were permitted structure/function claims). The petition thus calls on FDA to proceed down that slippery slope to greater censorship invited by the court in *Whitaker III*, increasingly carving out of the free speech market whole categories of truthful content and rendering that content the exclusive domain of the drug industry.

The real losers in this speech battle are consumers who--due to FDA's broad and expanding prior restraint on speech--are deprived of essential information concerning the therapeutic effects of certain nutrients they consume. Answering the call of the pharmaceutical industry for a monopoly on therapeutic claims, FDA has disingenuously led consumers to regard drugs, including those with severe side effects, as their only therapeutic options.

Although the legal battles over FDA censorship are far from over, FDA has proven itself on repeat occasions willing to violate the law. It violated constitutional limits on its authority no fewer than five times from 1999 to 2001. It has proven itself willing to censor health information even when that censorship leads to death and disability of the most vulnerable in our population, newborns (e.g., its multi-year refusal to allow a folic acid-neural tube defect claim despite 2,500 preventable neural tube defect births each year its censorship remained in place).

FDA has thus proven that it cannot be trusted to abide by decisions of the federal courts. Rather, it can be counted upon to achieve its desired end even if that end violates the Constitution and the orders of federal courts. The rule of law has been replaced by the rule of designing agency appointees. They operate outside the Constitution. They are unanswerable to the courts, the Congress, and the American people. They are possessed of so much power that they are never ultimately made to account for constitutional law violations or for the many lives and the property they choose to sacrifice.

7

FDA AND DEA DESTRUCTION OF COMPETITION

A drug is statutorily defined not by its physiological effect but by the claims made for it.[179] Thus, anything that is said to cure, mitigate, prevent, or treat a disease is a drug. The decision to define a drug by claims made for its use rather than by its biochemistry provides those who obtain new drug approval considerable market protection. Those so privileged enjoy FDA and patent protection from competition arising from knock-off products but also from unauthorized claims that are the same or substantially the same as claims FDA has approved for drugs.

By statutory design, the new drug approval process prevents any company from marketing a drug unless that company has obtained FDA approval.[180] Unlike the system for over-the-counter drugs, in the case of prescription drugs first approved by FDA and still under patent protection, no other party is permitted to produce a competing compound and market it without submitting and prosecuting to FDA approval a new drug application. The cost to bring a new drug to market exceeds $860 million, thus forming an insurmountable barrier to entry--making drug approval illusory for all but the wealthiest institutions in the world.

The enforcement authorities at FDA, through district offices across the country, spend much of their time policing the market to protect FDA approved drugs from competition.[181] They endeavor to find instances where drugs shipped for export or made by FDA approved drug manufacturers overseas and sold there at significantly lower prices are reimported into the United States. Such reimports, even when sponsored by state governments, are unlawful. FDA protects inflated domestic drug prices from competition derived from the very same drugs sold at below U.S. market prices overseas.

FDA also examines literature used to promote the sale of foods and dietary supplements to see if that literature includes an express or implied claim that the product treats or prevents disease. If a claim of that sort is found, the FDA declares the food or dietary supplement product an unapproved new drug by operation of law, forces it to be relabeled without therapeutic claims, or, if a party fails to comply, quarantines the product, obtains an injunction against its sale, and prosecutes the company that sells the product.[182] The prohibition on therapeutic claims applies irrespective of whether the claims are true.

By denying all others the right to sell chemical agents approved by FDA for sale by a specific company, and by denying all others the right to make therapeutic claims for natural substances, FDA achieves through force a competition free market for the sale of FDA approved drugs.

The Drug Enforcement Administration is a later entrant into the business of erecting barriers to competition. Over-the-counter drugs for the treatment of asthma and upper respiratory ailments contain ephedrine or pseudoephedrine. Ephedrine and pseudoephedrine are used in the making of illicit methamphetamines. Although over-the-counter cough and cold remedies are almost never used in the making of methamphetamines (representing less than 1% of the domestic source of the illicit drug), the DEA has made elimination of certain sources of cough and cold remedies an enforcement priority.[183]

Instances of "home cooks" making methamphetamine reveal that when cough and cold remedies are diverted for this use they are often obtained from pharmacies and big box stores, not convenience stores. The cost of the remedies in convenience stores is significantly higher than in the big box stores and the pharmacies. Moreover, even if all such remedies were eliminated from the market, there would likely be no effect on sale and use of methamphetamines because over 99% of demand for the illicit drug is supplied by finished drug products smuggled into the United States from Mexico and Canada.[184]

Of late, following meetings between the DEA Deputy Administrator and the pharmaceutical industry, DEA has embarked without the benefit of rulemaking on a systematic cleansing from the marketplace of all independent manufacturers and suppliers of cough and cold remedies to the convenience stores. Without any sound empirical evidence, DEA has taken the position that pharmacies, serviced by the major pharmaceutical companies, are not a source of diversion but that convenience stores, serviced by the independent pharmaceutical companies and their suppliers, are a common source for diversion of cough and cold remedies. DEA has prosecuted some fifty companies to revoke their registrations to sell those remedies.[185] Every one is an independent supplier of cough and cold remedies, and every one serves convenience stores or other non-chain pharmacy distribution sources.[186] DEA likewise has left the big box stores, also serviced by the major drug companies, free of enforcement.

The effect of DEA's selective enforcement is obviously anti-competitive. The DEA has allowed itself to be used as an agent for the largest pharmaceutical companies to rid the market of competition to their ephedrine and pseudoephedrine containing cough and cold remedies. It has destroyed some fifty companies, causing unemployment and significant economic hardship. The only institutions benefiting from this wholesale destruction of a segment of the market are the pharmaceutical companies that supply the pharmacies and big box stores. The enforcement activity has no effect on domestic supply or use of illicit methamphetamines.

8

CMS ELIMINATION OF INNOVATION IN MEDICINE

In an article for *Regulation* magazine, entitled "Murder by Medicare,"[187] I have before explained the stultifying effect Medicare's Byzantine labyrinth of regulation has on the practice of medicine in America. Representing over 100 physicians who must cope with Medicare, I am continually reminded of the fact that the insurance company contract carriers for Medicare, who determine whether a service is "medically reasonable and necessary," daily second guess the sound professional judgment of physicians, causing Medicare beneficiaries to suffer.

Physicians who treat Medicare beneficiaries worry constantly about whether the services they provide are ones that will be regarded by the insurance companies as routinely covered. They reasonably fear that if a service is not viewed as routine, it will trigger a Medicare audit. Consequently, the tendency is to provide a one-size-fits all treatment regimen for each disease, regardless of the patient's unique disease experience and need for exceptional care. Moreover, physicians must spend considerable time ensuring that their documentation of diagnoses and treatment meets Medicare standards because, in the end, that documentation will be all important.

The paperwork demands and the ever-present threat of an audit have turned the practice of medicine into a bureaucratic endeavor, where the physician's primary concern is self-preservation through diagnoses and prescription practices that please Medicare rather than the provision of a patient-centered service where the best interests of the patient dictate care. I have elsewhere referred to Medicare as "mediocre care" for that very reason.

Medicare is destroying quality medical care in the United States and is bureaucratizing it in a way that makes proposals of national health insurance appear to be Johnny come lately public announcements of a system already in place. Although Medicare is an enormous beast that invites much criticism, one aspect of the Medicare system reveals the horrific abuse of a federal agency given extraordinary legislative, executive, and judicial powers: How the Center for Medicare and Medicaid Services (CMS) treats physicians from whom it demands reimbursement under Medicare Part B.

Almost all Americans aged 65 and older are participants in Medicare Part B. Physicians who treat that population are thus deeply ensconced in the Medicare system. For them, Medicare reimbursement is essential and, yet, it is also far less than the market value for every service performed.

Medicare sets the amount to be paid for each service. Medicare determines largely on an ad hoc basis what services are medically reasonable and necessary and therefore compensable. Medicare expects physicians to remain ever cognizant (and legally presumes their knowledge) of the operational biases that characterize day to day decisions by Medicare's contract carriers, the insurance companies. The primary regulatees in the CMS system are the contract carriers, the insurance companies, that administer the program. CMS aims to influence the decisions of the insurance companies who implement the program but also to protect them against the ultimate CMS nemesis, the physicians.

Since the start of the Medicare program, Congress has bemoaned the astronomical costs of the program. Cost containment has become an incessant congressional demand, and CMS Administrators have been unsuccessful in containing costs except in one particular. Over the years, with the help of Congress, CMS has created traps for the unwary that ensnare hospitals, managed care organizations, and physicians and compel them to reimburse hundreds of millions of dollars to Medicare. That system was, at first, tied to acts of overt lawlessness, e.g., when physicians would submit claims for reimbursement of services never actually provided. Over time, and particularly with the passage of the Health Insurance Portability and Accountability Act of 1996, CMS has tied its reimbursement system to dozens of clever pitfalls that create a veritable mine field for physicians. If a physician fails to have adequate documentation for a service (even a service unquestionably necessary given the patient's actual symptoms), the absence of documentation justifies reimbursement to Medicare (and there is no medical file that cannot be found to lack some measure of documentation subjectively deemed necessary to support a claim for payment). If a physician provides a patient more service than CMS generally recognizes as compensable, then the provision of that greater than expected service, called "overutilization," justifies reimbursement to Medicare. If a physician provides a patient less service than CMS generally recognizes as compensable, then the physician may be considered to be guilty of "underutilization," a Medicare abuse. If a physician submitted a billing code for a service that was higher than the code the carrier believes appropriate for the patient, the physician is guilty of "upcoding," justifying reimbursement to Medicare. If a physician provides a patient a service covered by Medicare and a service not covered by Medicare and bills only for the covered service, the physician may nonetheless be denied coverage for the Medicare covered service on the argument that the covered service was ancillary to the non-covered. The potential grounds for reimbursement to Medicare are extensive and, for nearly all physicians, mind-boggling.

The insurance carriers who implement the Medicare program are largely protected from suit by federal law and precedent. Consequently they can make patently erroneous decisions and demand immediate compliance but the physician so victimized ordinarily has no legal recourse to prevent effectuation of the demand. The insurance carrier can pay claims for years without objection, only to require lump sum reimbursement thereafter yet suffer no liability for failing to require reimbursement in a timely fashion. In this way, a physician who maintains close contact with the insurance carrier (and receives regular assurance that his or her billing practices are appropriate) can be surprised when suddenly the carrier demands reimbursement of claims repeatedly paid. Indeed, false assurances from the carrier's agents to physicians do not relieve physicians of liability for reimbursement nor do they create liability for the carrier. The carrier is protected by federal law and precedent from liability for dispensing false information to physicians.

Before an insurance carrier demands reimbursement, it ordinarily performs an audit of the physician's patient files. That audit is of a subset of the physician's entire files for Medicare patients. From that subset, Medicare presumes any errors found in the sample to be characteristic of all Medicare billings made by the physician. It thus extrapolates and assigns a gross dollar amount for reimbursement equal to the amount that would be due and owing if all files contained the same rate of error as the sampled subset. Medicare applies a usurious interest rate to the amount demanded. Even before any binding decision against the physician, Medicare assesses the physician with reimbursement of the amount that would be due and owing if all files contained the same rate of error as the sampled subset plus interest at an annual rate that is comparable to that of a rip-off credit card. Every day that a physician does not pay, the amount due Medicare climbs. Within a matter of months, the amount demanded can be quite impressive. It is not uncommon for physicians from whom a sample reveals a $20,000 reimbursement liability to owe hundreds of thousands of dollars (due to the extrapolation) and then to owe tens of thousands atop that in interest.

When a physician sees a Medicare beneficiary, he must think not only of what his diagnosis and recommended treatment is but also of what Medicare will likely think of that diagnosis and recommended treatment. If, for example, in the physician's best medical judgment a patient has a disease of a certain complexity that would benefit from an extraordinary amount of care, the physician has to weigh whether provision of and billing for that extraordinary amount of care will increase his risk of being audited by Medicare. If that risk is reasonably likely in the mind of the physician or in the mind of risk managers working for a medical practice, clinic, or hospital, the physician may well either send the patient away to another, recommend a less extensive set of treatments, or exclude certain treatments altogether to reduce the risk.

When Medicare finally performs its audit and assigns liability, the physician must either pay the amount demanded plus interest, pay but fight, or not pay and fight. If the physician wants to challenge the carrier, he or she must be prepared for a multi-year contest that goes through a half dozen intra-CMS layers of review before the claim is ever presented to a court of law.[188] All the while, interest accrues on the amount demanded. The physician is thus placed in the position of either paying the amount demanded and quitting the fight or paying the amount demanded and fighting for its return in an environment designed to penalize that latter decision. The latter is quite obviously an unattractive proposition because to recoup just what the physician was paid for services requires legal fees that can easily enter the six figure category and beyond. Moreover, making the Medicare carrier displeased can lead to more audits, for which there is no lawful limit, and to more reimbursement demands. Furthermore, Medicare can deny reimbursement for all Medicare claims during the contest, so a physician, clinic, or hospital can be deprived of revenue needed to function and thus be forced to capitulate even when possessed of a winning case.

In the first instance, the physician must submit its grounds justifying Medicare reimbursement when presented with a demand for reimbursement from the Medicare carrier, the insurance company. At that juncture, the physician must make all arguments that will ever be allowed to be made in the entire case. While the physician is so limited, the carrier can make new arguments for denying reimbursement at every stage. If the grounds for reimbursement are rejected in the Medicare carrier's decision, the physician must then ask the carrier for a redetermination of that decision. If the redetermination is denied, then the physician must appeal to a Qualified Independent Carrier (QIC), another Medicare carrier, for a reconsideration of the claim decision. If that appeal is denied, then the physician must appeal to an HHS Administrative Law Judge. In the case before the Administrative Law Judge, the carrier and Medicare attorneys may appear but rarely if ever do because the ALJ is allowed to assume a prosecutorial role in addition to serving as judge. Thus, the ALJ often conducts cross-examination of witnesses. If the ALJ decides against the physician, the physician must then appeal to the Medicare Appeals Council (MAC) within HHS. That panel of four administrative law judges will then issue a decision. Among its options is a remand to the ALJ. Consequently, it is possible for the MAC to force a case to undergo several more months review before it can proceed on to a court. If the MAC decides against the physician, an appeal may finally be filed with the United States District

Court. The process of appeals before an independent court of law receives the case can take years, all the while the amount in issue continues to rise because of the exorbitant interest charged.

This system is grossly one-sided and unfair. It effectively presumes the accused guilty until proven innocent, and permits the imposition of draconian punishments upon the physician before a final decision in a court of law. In addition to the imposition of interest atop the amount demanded, HHS has the authority to refer the debt for action by the IRS, causing the IRS to withhold tax refunds, and the authority to suspend Medicare reimbursement payments. Moreover, HHS can place the accused physician on a national database accessible to insurance companies, licensing authorities in the states and the general public, displaying the unadjudicated charges against the physician without regard (or liability) for their defamatory impact.

This system favors CMS's principal regulatee, its contract carriers, at the expense of the physicians it is required to pay and the patients it is supposed to serve. The result is a mediocre system of socialized medicine that dumbs down the care provided by and ratchets up the risks associated with the practice of medicine. The combination of the two has created a huge disincentive that may in part be responsible for the shortage of physicians in certain specialties and parts of the country and for the progressive destruction of solo and small group medical practices.

9

THE WAY BACK TO LIBERTY

Montesquieu observed:

> When a republic has been corrupted, none of the ills that arise can be remedied except by removing the corruption and recalling the principles; every other correction is either useless or a new ill. So long as Rome preserved its principles, judgments could be in the hands of the senators without suffering abuse; but when it had been corrupted, regardless of the body to which judgments were transferred, whether to senators, knights, or public treasurers, or to two of these bodies, to all three together, or to any other body at all, the result was always bad. Knights had no more virtue than senators, public treasurers no more than knights, and the latter as little as centurions.[189]

Elected officials have relinquished their power to govern. They have been complicit in industry take-over of the independent regulatory agencies and commissions to which they have imparted governing power; they have done virtually nothing to prevent that take-over and, aware of it, do nothing to stop it. They have avoided any true reforms that would halt or reverse either their abdication of the power to govern or industry take-over of the agencies and commissions. By doing nothing, they have effectively facilitated or condoned actions by the agencies and commissions that grant market protection to favored industry leaders brought about through adoption of regulations that block market entry or decrease existing competition.

The abdication of constitutional function has arisen in some cases because of a benign ignorance or negligence on the part of members of Congress. In other instances, it has been part of corrupt deal-making by members, whereby they sacrifice the Constitution, permit an effective raid on public coffers, or sacrifice the property or liberty rights of certain businesses or individuals in exchange for lucrative paybacks from the companies benefited by the legislative action or inaction (benefits that are often in the form of future employment).

Appointed officials have allowed the agencies and commissions that they head to become the captives of industry leaders. In certain instances, as in the case of the Food and Drug Administration, the take-over by industry is so complete that it is an unremarkable and common observation that the industry controls virtually every important decision made by the agency. Industry has achieved the takeovers as part of a quid-pro-quo wherein the agency or commission acquires some new regulatory power in exchange for market protection and above rates of return for favored regulatees.

Those appointed to run agencies and commissions have an inherent conflict of interest. They are aware that the decisions they make will either please or displease favored regulatees. They are aware that their decisions will either enhance or diminish their prospects for employment and business opportunity when they leave government. So, for example, a commissioner of the Federal Communications Commission knows that if he or she votes in favor of agency action that offends the interests of the major broadcast, cable, and telecommunications companies, he or she can expect that those companies and their Washington area law and lobbying firms will not be sources of future gainful employment when that Commissioner enters the private sector. The same is true for the commissioners of the Federal Trade Commission. The effect extends beyond market positions to financed chairs at universities. Can the Commissioner of the Food and Drug Administration or a commissioner of the Federal Trade Commission expect to have a chair in a major university's department of medicine or economics if the endowment for that chair is financed by a company that did not fair well in agency decisionmaking? Thus, it is that the future of those appointed to assume regulatory positions in the agencies and commissions is affected by the decisions they make in those positions. That reality colors everything they do.

The abdication of constitutional governing power (the Congress's delegation of core law-making powers to independent regulatory agencies and commissions and those agencies and commissions' effective turn-over of governing power to the industries they were created to regulate) is widespread and has transformed our limited federal republic into a bureaucratic oligarchy that works day to day to elevate the economic prospects of favored regulatees at the expense of others disenfranchised.

Beginning in earnest in the 1930s and continuing to the present, the nation's governing power has been for sale to those with economic wherewithal, persistence, and political clout who are willing to finance the payroll and retirement of elected and appointed officials. Elected officials have proven themselves willing to sell their governing power to industry either directly (as in the case of the Medicare Prescription Drug Improvement and Modernization Act of 2003) or indirectly as when members do nothing (other than complain in hearings or in letters to the agencies concerning industry favoritism and related internal corruption) to stop industry takeover of regulatory commissions and agencies.

Americans must come to the realization that the Congress of the United States and the agencies and commissions of the federal government are infected with a corruption born of the self-interest of those in power and the infection is widespread. They must come to realize that the regulatory state has been an abysmal failure because it has ceded governing control to industry, has witnessed industry use regulation as a vehicle to create barriers to competition, block competition, and punish competitors, and has even given a large part of the nation's purse to the biggest monopoly government has ever created, the pharmaceutical industry.

The founders understood that with power comes corruption. They knew that the only way to reduce or eliminate corruption in government was to reduce or eliminate the power of governors. It is not the case that if we change who sits in Congress or who sits in the agencies we will solve this problem. While in a single instance a person of good conscience might avoid making a decision that sacrifices life, liberty, and property, the fact that the power to sacrifice those inalienable rights exists in the office means that sooner or later a person will come along who will use the power. It also means that every person who occupies that office will realize that the choices made will affect his or her own future employment prospects.

The Constitution's separation of powers and non-delegation doctrines were designed to create institutional limits on abuses of power. Unfortunately, those doctrines have become part of what Judge Ginsberg refers to as the "Constitution in exile." Without fundamental reforms to breathe life into those doctrines we will not be able to resurrect the government of limited and checked powers that the founders entrusted to us. We will instead continue to witness the rise of tyranny and the loss of liberty.

Unquestionably we must start the movement back to good government by removing those many corrupt individuals who now occupy positions of power in Congress and in the administrative agencies and commissions. We must replace them with others committed to supplanting the bureaucratic oligarchy that presently rules us with the limited federal republic the Constitution prescribes.

Voting Corrupt Members of Congress Out of Office

We must determine who in Congress has been responsible for the ceding of governing control to the agencies and commissions. Who has voted in favor of bills that give new regulatory powers or enormous sums to agencies with vacuous directives that permit those agencies to act at will and thus pervert public resources to do the bidding of industry leaders? We will find that a super majority of both houses, and of Democratic and Republican stripe, have voted in favor of those bills. Americans must vote those members out of office. We must demand from those who seek elected office a commitment to restore the limited federal republic the Constitution prescribes, to take back legislative power from the agencies and to limit the influence of industry over Congress and the agencies. Congress must help dismantle the regulatory state, so that core functions are performed by Congress directly or by institutions under the direct control of Congress. We must not be fooled by those who offer reforms that do nothing to dismantle the regulatory state or to return legislative power to Congress. Measures that require disclosure of lobbyists or amounts contributed to campaigns, and measures that limit access of lobbyists to Congress or agencies are of limited utility and do not address the penultimate separation, and delegation, of powers issues that have robbed us of constitutional government.

Enacting Legislation to Prevent Congressional Relinquishment of the Law-Making Power

On behalf of Congressman Ron Paul of Texas, I drafted a bill entitled the Congressional Responsibility and Accountability Act. That bill would effectively reverse substantive delegation of law-making power from Congress to the independent agencies and commissions by preventing the adoption of any agency rule that has an economic impact unless and until Congress has enacted the rule into law. In other words, the regulatory state would not be able to create law affecting the economy without Congress taking on its constitutional role of enacting the law in question. I have defined the economic impact that triggers the need for Congressional enactment to arise when any proposed agency or commission rule would (1) impose a cost on an individual of $5,000 or more in a year; (2) impose a cost on any business entity of $25,000 or more in a year; (3) impose a cost on all Americans (i.e., the economy in general) of $250,000 in a year; or (4) cause 1 American citizen or more to lose employment in a year. Existing rules having these impacts would be rendered legally unenforceable until such time, if ever, as Congress enacted them.

Enacting Legislation to Prevent Industry Capture

As explained above, the federal regulatory commissions and agencies have become captives of industry. The effect has been a near constant promulgation and enforcement of rules that restrict competition, reduce economic opportunity, reduce the availability of goods and services, and increase costs to consumers. The effect has also been to abdicate law-making power to favored industry regulatees. In the case of the drug industry, the FDA has ceded so much control over the drug approval process to the industry that FDA regularly approves drugs that its own medical reviewers have defined as unsafe and as likely to cause significant loss of life or permanent disability. Thus, Vioxx entered the market and killed some 55,000 Americans (comparable to the number that were killed in the Vietnam war); Ketek, Serevent, Rezulin, Redux, and a dozen others have entered the market causing scores to die and many more to suffer serious debilitating injuries.

Nothing in the law stands in the way of repeat occurrences. We may thus expect into the foreseeable future that FDA will continue to approve for marketing drugs that the evidence indicates will impose risks that vastly exceed any provable benefit. As FDA Associate Director of the Office of Drug Safety Dr. David J. Graham has stated, FDA is "incapable of protecting America against another Vioxx . . . We are virtually defenseless."

Preventing industry capture requires a shift away from reliance on a regulatory state where unelected oligarchs are given virtually unbridled discretion to enact law. It also requires members of Congress to vote without regard to the economic benefits specific industry leaders or organizations will bestow upon them. Those corrupt practices must come to an end if we are to be, and remain, a free people.

We need to enact legislation that forbids appointment of any person to an office in an agency or commission who has previously worked for a regulatee of that agency or commission. We must also prohibit for life any appointed agency official from accepting payment, employment, positions of distinction, or gifts of any kind from any regulatee (or any organization to which the regulatee makes a financial contribution).

We need to enact legislation that prohibits for life any member of Congress who receives a financial contribution from, or who votes in favor of a bill that provides an economic benefit to, any specific individual, company, or industry from accepting payment, employment, positions of distinction, or gifts of any kind from that individual, company, or industry at any time in the future.

Enacting Legislation to Require Meaningful Federal Judicial Review

We need to amend the Administrative Procedure Act to define anew the standard of judicial review used in determining the legality of any agency or commission action. Presently those actions are upheld in almost every case because the Supreme Court has required judicial deference to agency interpretation of enabling statutes. Under the governing law in *Chevron U.S.A. Inc. v. Natural Resources Defense Council*,[190] a federal court must broadly defer to any agency interpretation of its statutory authority unless that interpretation is manifestly contrary to the plain language of the agency's enabling statute. The *Chevron* court ruled:

> If Congress has explicitly left a gap for the agency to fill, there is an express delegation of authority to the agency to elucidate a specific provision of the statute by regulation. Such legislative regulations are given controlling weight unless they are arbitrary, capricious, or manifestly contrary to the statute. Sometimes the legislative delegation to an agency on a particular question is implicit rather than explicit. In such a case, a court may not substitute its own construction of a statutory provision for a reasonable interpretation made by the administrator of an agency.[191]

Chevron ushered in an era of broad deference to administrative agency action, one where the onus is against employing any serious scrutiny of the action to discern the extent to which that action satisfies not only the letter of the law but also the intended meaning of the law.

Through amendment Congress needs to provide a new standard for review of all administrative agency actions. The present statutory law prohibits administrative agency action that violates the Constitution or the laws of the United States or is otherwise arbitrary and capricious or an abuse of discretion. The language needs to be amended to provide the following for use in federal judicial review. In assessing whether the agency action complies with the laws of the United States, the agency must establish that Congress has expressly authorized the action the agency has taken through unambiguous statutory language and through express legislative intent concerning that language. No administrative agency action shall be upheld by a federal court as lawful unless it is authorized by the unambiguous terms of the agency's enabling statute and is consistent with the express intent of Congress.

Enacting Legislation to Punish Appointed Officials Who Violate the Constitution, Agency Rules, or Commission Enabling Statutes for Personal Gain

We need to enact legislation that requires the Attorney General to prosecute any appointed official upon receipt of evidence that the official ordered the taking of an action that violated the Constitution of the United States, an order of a federal court, or an Agency or Commission's enabling statute or rule and thereafter took custody of any thing of economic value from one or more regulatees that benefited from the action. The penalty should be a mandatory minimum ten year prison term and a requirement that an amount equal to the fair market value of the thing of value received be paid pro rata to the parties (including the estates of the deceased) that suffered a loss of life, property, or civil liberties as a result of the action. If the appointed official is still in office, the legislation would require an initial prosecution by the Attorney General to remove the official from office and then permit the Attorney General to prosecute for the offense. If the Attorney General elects not to prosecute within thirty days of the date the official is removed from office, then the statute should permit private causes of action against the former official by those who have suffered financial losses with an entitlement to a civil penalty awardable to the plaintiffs consisting of the fair market value of the thing of value received atop legal fees associated with bringing and prosecuting the action.

The legislation would require proof that the former official acted in violation of the Constitution or the agency's enabling statute or rule *and* took custody of a thing of value from a party who benefited from the law violation. Ordinarily the financial gain will come after the official has left office. There should be no limit on the time of receipt of that financial gain or statute of limitation on the bringing of the suit.

Enacting Legislation to Protect the Public from Unsafe Drugs

There can be no question that the present FDA is controlled by the pharmaceutical industry and that internal agency reforms will not change the political dynamic that keeps Commissioners beholden to the pharmaceutical industry. The Congress of the United States has also demonstrated that it has no will to end pharmaceutical industry control of the agency; indeed, many, if not most, in Congress willingly preserve the status quo to keep the pharmaceutical industry in control at the agency. The Associate Director of FDA's Office of Drug Safety succinctly identifies the problem:

> ... FDA has a well-established history of suppressing its scientists, of pressuring them to change their recommendations and conclusions if they are unfavorable about a drug and retaliation against those scientists who don't buckle under FDA pressure and threats. FDA calls itself the world's leading consumer protection agency. If the public only knew the truth, they'd demand that Congress fix the problem. Of course, Congress has no intention of doing anything that would upset the industry either. What has emerged is a lethal triangle involving FDA, the pharmaceutical industry and Congress. Pharmaceutical money funds FDA and exerts great influence with Congress. FDA allows deadly drugs onto the market and Congress pretends that nothing is the matter.

Legislation needs to be introduced removing from FDA the power to determine drug safety and efficacy. FDA's legacy of censorship of science, duplicity, and approval of unsafe drugs has proven the agency, regardless of who Congress has chosen to run it, entirely incapable of reliably protecting the public from unsafe drugs. FDA suffers from a pervasive corruption in which the instruments of governance are under the control of its principal regulatees.

By statute, Congress should create a system to qualify university departments of pharmacy, pharmacology, biology, and biochemistry to serve as independent reviewers of drug applications. Under such a system, a drug company would file an application for a new drug with the Department of Justice. DOJ would be required to prepare a copy of the application that removes all reference express or implied to the drug company sponsor such that it would be impossible to discern the sponsor. The application would then be given at random to any one of a number of universities that had applied for and received approval by DOJ to be reviewing institutions. The statute would prescribe all elements necessary to qualify a reviewing institution and DOJ would determine whether qualifications were met. Each institution would be barred from receiving any funding directly or indirectly from the drug company sponsor and each review would be required to take place anonymously such that neither the drug company sponsor nor the institution reviewing the application would be aware of the other. The statute would need to provide the institution with immunity from suit by the drug company sponsor. The review would assess the extent to which the drug agents in issue cause safety risks and would make the penultimate biomedical determination of whether the safety risks present exceed the putative benefits of the drug. The institution would have to decide based on the evidence presented to it and its own testing of the drug and would be required to issue a single, final decision no later than 16 months after receipt of the application. The institution's decision on safety would be dispositive, deemed a decision of the United States, and could only be challenged by suit in federal district court, not before the FDA, within thirty days of the decision. The decision would be released by the institution to the public when final. The company sponsor could challenge the decision in federal court naming the United States as a party. The FDA would be obliged to defend the institution decision, and the institution could participate as an intervenor at its election with the cost of the institution's participation being paid for by the FDA.

The onus would be on the company sponsor to establish that the review decision failed to take into account facts or circumstances that prove the product to be safer than recited in the institution's decision. A court would decide whether evidence of a lack of safety exceeded evidence of benefit and, if so, would affirm. If not, it would reverse. The Court would be given the statutory option sua sponte or at the request of any party to require a limited court monitored market release of the product on an experimental basis for up to a year to determine whether in fact risks exceed benefits. The institution and DOJ could return to court at any time during the marketing of the product if evidence of a lack of safety presented a risk of death or serious injury to patients and could obtain an injunction to halt sale and distribution on an expedited basis in the presence of such proof. A system of this kind would divorce the process from FDA internal politics and industry favoritism and would ensure that the initial determination was predicated to the maximum extent possible on medical and scientific proof.

Enacting Legislation to Eliminate FDA Jurisdiction Over Health Claims and Structure/Function Claims and Establish New Anti-Fraud Protections

Legislation needs to be introduced removing jurisdiction from FDA over health and structure/function claims. The speech police at FDA need to be disarmed and reassigned. Through its prior restraint on health claims, FDA has censored truthful nutrient-disease information for over half a century. The government has deprived consumers of their right to receive information at the point of sale that can enable them to discern the physiological effects of foods and supplements and thereby exercise informed choice.

Through its repeated reclassification of permitted structure/function claims to prohibited drug claims, FDA is working to remove whole categories of speech from the food and dietary supplement market and reserve those categories for the exclusive use of its favored regulatee, the pharmaceutical industry. That censorship likewise robs the public of vital health information needed to make informed choices.

FDA censorship has kept vital information concerning the effects of nutrients on health and disease from the public. It has thereby contributed to hundreds of thousands of deaths and disabilities (from, among others, preventable neural tube defects (folic acid) to preventable sudden death heart attacks (omega-3 fatty acids)).

FDA has repeatedly defied constitutional mandates from the federal courts to favor disclosure over suppression. It has created a de facto health information monopoly for drugs, including those with dire side effects, to the exclusion of specific dietary supplements and foods that have therapeutic effects without toxicity.

The prior restraint on health claims is an historic anomaly, a throw-back to the dreaded Fourteenth through Seventeenth Century Courts of Star Chamber in England, a system rejected by the Constitution's founders. Prior restraints were never to regain a foothold in this country so long as the First Amendment remained the law of the land. The prior restraint on health claims was created and is maintained for the purpose of providing the pharmaceutical industry a monopoly on the right to communicate therapeutic information. In other words, it is an anti-competitive device employed by FDA at the behest of the pharmaceutical industry. The notion that it protects against fraud in the market is a largely false justification, a cover for the real purpose which is anti-competitive.

Prior restraints are loathsome because they apply to all, not just to those who purvey falsehoods. Consequently, the ban on health claims robs the American marketplace of virtually all of the hundreds of thousands of peer-reviewed, university based findings on the effects of nutrients. The ban is predicated on the illogical argument that through a categorical prohibition on all speech the government arrests that subset of speakers who depend upon fraud to sell their goods. Fraud is illegal, of course, regardless of the existence of the health claim prior restraint. Consequently, those who defraud are most often doing so cognizant of the fact that they are committing a law violation separate and apart from the health claim prior restraint. The presence of a law that prohibits all speech of a certain category from being communicated has no effect upon those already engaged (and willing to engage) in unlawful conduct. The illegality of the fraud pre-exists the prior restraint and the tools to enforce the prior restraint are applied selectively, not universally. Consequently, the only people who feel obliged to avoid communication in the category banned are those who are law-abiding, precisely the ones who would speak responsibly and aid consumers in the marketplace. As a result, the prior restraint on health claims has had very little effect on the presence of fraud in the food and dietary supplement markets but has succeeded in silencing those who would educate the public of advances in nutrition science.

By amendment to the Food Drug and Cosmetic Act, Congress needs to deny FDA any jurisdiction over health claims and structure/function claims. To ensure that the law does not impose a loathsome prior restraint (always a bane to liberty) and is properly tailored to reach the subset of fraudulent speakers, Congress should adopt new legislation to punish fraud in the market communication of health information. That new legislation should place the burden of proof on the government to establish the falsity of health information used in the market upon empirical evidence, not conjecture. If the statement is found to be false by a United States District Court but not likely to cause physical harm, then the remedy should be limited to (1) an injunction against the marketing of the product in question with the false health information, (2) a requirement that the marketer publish in the same venues previously used to advertise a clear statement that the health information it used to market the product was false, and (3) a requirement that the marketer reimburse the sale price of the product to all of those who purchased it in reliance on the false information. If the health information is found to be false and likely to cause physical harm, then the remedy should be equal to that for the communication of false information not likely to cause physical harm plus a term of incarceration for the parties responsible.

In determining whether false health information is likely to cause physical harm, the government should be required to bear the burden of proof to establish (1) that qualified experts have determined that the health information when used to market the product is likely to cause physical harm and (2) that the typical person who markets comparable products would understand use of the false health information to create a risk of physical harm such that the harm would be reasonably foreseeable. The term of imprisonment should be calculated based on the perceived degree of culpability of the parties charged and on the extent of injury actually caused or likely to be caused by the false health information. Until the law is so amended, and is revised as recommended above to remove FDA from the business of determining the safety and efficacy of drugs, Congress should enact the Health Freedom Protection Act. I wrote that bill at the behest of Congressman Ron Paul. It would require FDA to implement the First Amendment protective standard of *Whitaker v. Thompson* I, and it would place the burden of proof on the government to establish the falsity of claims before banning them. It would also eliminate "implied claims" enforcement and it would overrule FDA and allow several nutrient-disease relationship claims for which the evidence is overwhelming, including the glucosamine-chondroitin sulfate-osteoarthritis risk reduction claim, to enter the market.

 We must end the current draconian system of FDA prior restraints. We must replace FDA's creation of a drug company monopoly on therapeutic information with a free market in health information. That new free market, although free of prior restraints, should be tempered by law enforcement to arrest those who abuse their freedom to communicate false health information to the public. The system recommended here fulfills, rather than violates, the First Amendment and replaces a legacy of FDA speech suppression that has sacrificed life and health with one that will promote health freedom.

Enacting Legislation to Mandate Due Process in Medicare Part B Reimbursement Cases

Legislation needs to be introduced that removes from Medicare the authority to judge appeals from its carrier's reimbursement decisions and permits those appeals to be placed directly in the federal courts. The very first appeal from a carrier decision should be to a court of law to ensure an unbiased review and an expedited decision. In addition, the law should prohibit the assessment of interest except in instances where a court finds the physician to have received actual notice from the carrier that billing for the service or services in question was not permitted and to have billed for those services despite the notice. Moreover, the law should include a presumption against reimbursement if the carrier failed to demand reimbursement from a physician within one year of Medicare's payment of a bill, and the carrier should be prohibited from seeking reimbursement from the physician for any amounts paid if reimbursement is sought after three years from the first date of Medicare's payment of a bill for a particular service, except in instances of fraud. Finally, if a physician prevails against Medicare, the party responsible for making an erroneous demand for reimbursement (whether it is the carrier or it is HHS directly or both) should be required to pay the physician for his or her legal fees incurred in pursuit of reimbursement.

Making the foregoing changes will remove from the present system its onerous and inequitable pre-judgment penalties and will lessen the time for ultimate decision. The changes will remove bias from the decision-making process by preventing prosecutors (the contract carriers and the HHS ALJs) from being judges. The changes will also place significant new pressure on the contract carriers to avoid making reimbursement demands absent good cause for so doing.

EPILOGUE

With equal force today we may say as President Reagan did in his first Inaugural Address, "In this present crisis, government is not the solution to our problem; government is the problem."[192] The private sector engine responsible for all innovation, for the taxes that run the government, and for our nation's standard of living quakes under the overwhelming weight of anti-competitive regulations. Those regulations have been heaped upon the market by unelected officials who seek financial rewards from the industries benefited and who care little for the liberty and lives lost as a result of their actions. As Judge Laurence H. Ginsberg presciently observed, the key doctrines that protect us from concentrations of power form a Constitution-in-exile. Our government is dominated by the industry it supposedly regulates. The unelected heads of the regulatory agencies, possessed of the very powers in single hands that the founders forbad, discriminate against new market entrants in favor of industry incumbents and then reap the spoils from industry leaders in lucrative post-government positions funded by those leaders. Members of Congress responsible for the broad delegations of legislative, executive, and judicial powers from the 1930s to the present are themselves frequent beneficiaries of industry largesse and are participants in the same corruption that riddles the bureaucracy.

Our great nation is brought low by actions that sacrifice the lives, liberties, and property of the many to benefit the few in power. The reverse of this long sordid decline from a limited federal republic to an unlimited bureaucratic oligarchy depends, as it always has, on a vigilant public willing to throw out the rascals in Washington who contribute to the decline and put in their place patriotic souls who will do what is necessary to restore the republic.

We are at a critical moment in history. Corruption within the government is pervasive and there are virtually no checks on the abuses. We must either reverse the trend toward ruin promptly or stand by as we lose our place as a bastion of liberty, hope, and opportunity for the world. The founders understood that just governments are instituted among men to protect the rights of the governed and that wherever political power is concentrated there lies the greatest danger to liberty. The founders looked to us to "preserve the sacred fire of liberty." They made preservation of liberty a solemn trust to be passed from generation to generation. They understood that their handiwork, the Constitution, would be but a mere parchment barrier against a people intent on bringing down that barrier in pursuit of self-interest. George Washington foretold present dangers early in the life of the Republic when in his September 17, 1796 Farewell Address, he warned:

> The necessity of reciprocal checks in the exercise of political power, by dividing and distributing it into different depositaries, and constituting each the guardian of the public weal against invasions by the others, has been evinced by experiments ancient and modern; some of them in our country and under our own eyes. To preserve them must be as necessary as to institute them. If, in the opinion of the people, the distribution or modification of the con-

stitutional powers be in any particular wrong, let it be corrected by an amendment in the way which the Constitution designates. But let there be no change by usurpation; for though this, in one instance, may be the instrument of good, it is the customary weapon by which free governments are destroyed.

If that love of liberty that has inspired great Americans to sacrifice all to secure its blessings can be translated into political action in our day, we may yet see a restoration of the republic and a rekindling of liberty's sacred fire.

NOTES

INTRODUCTION

1. THE FEDERALIST NO. 47, at 303 (James Madison, Alexander Hamilton, & John Jay) (Isaac Kramnick ed., Penguin Books 1987).
2. Thomas Jefferson, *Notes on the state of Virginia*, Query 13, 120-121 (1784).
3. Thomas Jefferson, *Notes on the state of Virginia*, Query 13, 120-121 (1784).

CHAPTER ONE

4. There are rich English antecedents to the separation of powers doctrine. For example, John Trenchard (who with Thomas Gordon wrote under the pseudonym Cato a series of 144 letters on liberty published in the *London Journal* from 1720 to 1723 and republished in the colonies) described the essential need for separation of powers to guard against tyranny in Trenchard's *A Short History of Standing Armies in England* (1698):

    "All wise governments endeavor, as much as possible, to keep the *legislative* and *executive parts* asunder, that they may be a check upon one another. Our government trusts the King with no part of the *legislative* but a *negative voice*, which is absolutely necessary to preserve the *executive*. One part of the duty of the *House of Commons* is to punish offenders and redress the grievances occasioned by the *executive* part of the government; and how can that be done if they should happen to be the *same persons*, unless they would be public-spirited enough to *hang* or *drown themselves*?"

    Quoted by Bolingbroke in VI *Craftsman* No. 198 (London, 1731) 142. Cato's Letters were "were republished entire or in part again and again, 'quoted in every colonial newspaper from Boston to Savannah,' and referred to repeatedly in the pamphlet literature" because they were esteemed "the most authoritative statement of the nature of political liberty." Bernard Bailyn, *The Ideological Origins of the American Revolution* 36 (Belknap Press, Harvard University Press 1967); *see also* John Locke, *Two Treatises of Government* 2d Treatise, §§ 143, 144, 150, 159 (Peter Laslett ed., Mentor Books 1965) (1689).

5. THE FEDERALIST NO. 47, at 303 (James Madison, Alexander Hamilton, & John Jay) (Isaac Kramnick ed., Penguin Books 1987).
6. Excerpted in 1 THE FOUNDERS' CONSTITUTION 443 (Philip B. Kurland and Ralph Lerner eds.) (1987).
7. "Instructions of the Inhabitants of the Town of Boston to Their Representatives in Congress" excerpted in 1 THE FOUNDERS' CONSTITUTION 319 (Philip B. Kurland & Ralph Lerner eds.) (1987).
8. Montesquieu, *The Spirit of the Laws* 157 (Cohler, Miller & Stone eds., Cambridge University Press 2000).
9. John Adams, *Thoughts on Government, in* THE PAPERS OF JOHN ADAMS 4:86-93 (Robert J. Taylor et al. eds., Belknap Press, Harvard University Press 1977) (1776).
10. Thomas Jefferson, *Notes on the state of Virginia*, Query 13, 120-121 (1784).
11. THE FEDERALIST NO. 4, at 309, 312 (James Madison, Alexander Hamilton, & John Jay) (Isaac Kramnick ed., Penguin Books 1987). "Will it be sufficient to mark, with precision, the boundaries of these departments in the constitution of the government, and to trust to these parchment barriers against the encroaching spirit of power? This is the security which appears to have been principally relied on by the compilers of most of the American constitutions. But experience assures us that the efficacy of the provision has been greatly overrated; and that some more adequate defense is indispensably necessary for the more feeble against the more powerful members of the government." *Id.* at 309.
12. Montesquieu, *The Spirit of the Laws* 155 (Cohler, Miller & Stone eds., Cambridge University Press 2000).
13. THE FEDERALIST NO. 4, at 309 (James Madison, Alexander Hamilton, & John Jay) (Isaac Kramnick ed., Penguin Books 1987).
14. *See supra* note 4.
15. Excerpted in 1 THE FOUNDERS' CONSTITUTION 55 (Philip B. Kurland & Ralph Lerner eds., 1987).
16. Excerpted in 1 THE FOUNDERS' CONSTITUTION 142 (Philip B. Kurland & Ralph Lerner eds., 1987).

17. Quoted in 1 THE FOUNDERS' CONSTITUTION 477 (Philip B. Kurland & Ralph Lerner eds., 1987).
18. Thomas Jefferson, *Kentucky Resolutions* (1798).
19. *See* Nicholas J. Szabo, *Origins of the Non-Delegation Doctrine*, Seminar Paper, the George Washington University Law School, at 15, *available at*, http://szabo.best.vwh.net/delegation.pdf.
20. George Washington, Farewell Address (1796).
21. 467 U.S. 837 (1984).
22. Whitman v. Am. Trucking Ass'ns, 531 U.S. 457, 474 (2001) ("In the history of the Court we have found the requisite 'intelligible principle' lacking in only two statutes, one of which provided literally no guidance for the exercise of discretion, and the other of which conferred authority to regulate the entire economy by assuring 'fair competition'").
23. Whitman, 531 U.S. at 473 (2001).

CHAPTER TWO

24. David Schoenbrod, *Power Without Responsibility: How Congress Abuses the People Through Delegation* 10 (Yale University Press, 1993).
25. Schoenbrad, *supra* note 24, at 17.
26. Quoted in Schoenbrod, *supra* note 24, at 38: "Bonito Mussolini, whom Roosevelt referred to in 1933 as that 'admirable Italian gentleman,' remarked upon hearing of the NIRA, 'Ecco un ditatore!' ('Behold a dictator!')."
27. Louisville Joint Stock Land Bank v. Radford, 296 U.S. 661 (1935).
28. Humphrey's Executor v. United States, 295 U.S. 602 (1935).
29. Schechter Poultry Corp v. United States, 295 U.S. 495 (1935).
30. United States v. Butler, 2297 U.S. 1 (1935).
31. Carter v. Carter Coal Co., 298 U.S. 238 (1936).
32. Morehead v. New York ex rel. Tipaldo, 298 U.S. 587 (1936).
33. Schechter, 295 U.S. at 529.
34. Those Justices were Willis Van Devanter; James McReynolds; George Sutherland; and Pierce Butler (who strongly opposed the New Deal programs) and Charles Evans Hughes (the Chief Justice) and Owen Roberts (who had voted against the programs on occasion). The three justices who had voted in favor of the consti-

tutionality of the programs were Louis D. Brandeis; Harlan Fiske Stone; and Benjamin Cardozo.

35. For a detailed review of this struggle between the Executive and the Court, see Leonard Baker, *Back to Back: The Duel between FDR and the Supreme Court* (New York: Macmillan, 1967), and William Leuchtenburg, *The Origins of Franklin D. Roosevelt's 'Court-Packing Plan,'* SUPREME COURT REVIEW 347-400 (1966).
36. Bernard H. Siegan, *Economic Liberties and the Constitution* 3-4 (University of Chicago Press, 1980).
37. Douglas H. Ginsburg, "Delegation Running Riot," a review of *Power Without Responsibility: How Congress Abuses the People through Delegation* by David Schoenbrod, REGULATION (1995), *available at*, www.cato.org/pubs/regulation/reg18n1f.html.
38. David E. Lewis, *Presidents and the Politics of Agency Design: Political Insulation in the United States Government Bureaucracy, 1946-1997* at 42-44 (Stanford University Press, 2003).
39. *See* Ian Fleming, *You Only Live Twice* (1964).

CHAPTER THREE

40. *See* George J. Stigler, *The theory of economic regulation*, BELL J. ECON. MAN. SCI. 2:3-21 (1971).
41. Gordon Tullock, *The Welfare Costs of Tariffs, Monopolies, and Theft*, 5 W. ECON. J. 224-232 (1967).
42. Sanford Ikeda, "Rent-Seeking: A Primer," 53 (11) *The Freeman* (Nov. 2003).
43. *See* National Institute for Health Care Management Foundation, *Prescription Drugs and Intellectual Property Protection: Finding the Right Balance Between Access and Innovation* at 10 (2000).
44. Alastair J.J. Wood, "A Proposal for Radical Changes in the Drug-Approval Process," 355 NEW ENG. J. MED. 618 (Aug. 10, 2006).
45. Steve Goldstein, "U.S. prescription drug sales growth slowed to 3.8% in 2007," WALL ST. J. DIGITAL WATCH, (MarketWatch, March 12, 2008), *at* http://www.marketwatch.com/news/story/us-prescription-drug-sales-growth/story.aspx?guid=%7B37AD0634-681C-4E1A-AC1F-E364D027B3C9%7D (last visited July 30, 2008).
46. *See* Marcia Angell, *The Truth About the Drug Companies* 142 (Random House, 2004).

47. *See* Angell, *supra* note 46, at 115; *see also* John Abramson, *Overdosed America* (Harper Collins, 2004) at 124:

> Anyone who has spent any time in a doctor's office will have noticed the constant parade of attractive and well-dressed drug company sales representatives giving away trinkets to the staff and trying desperately to get a moment of the doctor's time. The number of reps making sales pitches in doctors' offices has *tripled* over the past 10 years. There is now one full-time drug rep for every four and a half office-based doctors. In 2001, drug companies spent $4.7 billion "detailing" ("industry speak" for drug reps' sales calls) to the 490,000 office-based doctors in the United States, or about $10,000 for each doctor per year. And that doesn't include the cost of the drug samples the reps left.

48. *See, e.g.*, Abramson, *supra* note 47, at 94-95; 196-197; 252-253; 25-27; 37-38; 93-94; 96-97; Angell, *supra* note 46, at 100-106.
49. *See, e.g.*, Abramson, *supra* note 47, at 111 ("From the moment doctors enter medical school to the moment they retire, drug companies and medical-device manufacturers attempt to influence their medical decisions").
50. *See* Abramson, *supra* note 47, at Chapters 2, 3, 7, 8.
51. *See* "Under The Influence," CBS NEWS.COM (July 29, 2007), *at* http://www.cbsnews.com/stories/2007/03/29/60minutes/printable2 625305.shtml (last visited July 30, 2008).
52. *See* M. Asif Ismail, "A Record Year for the Pharmaceutical Lobby in '07 (Washington's largest lobby racks up another banner year on Capitol Hill)," CENTER FOR PUBLIC INTEGRITY, *available at*, http://projects.publicintegrity.org/rx/report.aspx?aid=985 (last visited July 30, 2008).
53. *See Medicare Part D patients pay more for drugs than veterans*, ARIZONA DAILY STAR (Jan. 10. 2007), *available at*, http://www.azstarnet.com/sn/printDS/163911 (last visited July 30, 2008).
54. *See* ARIZONA DAILY STAR, *supra* note 53.
55. *See* CBS NEWS.COM, *supra* note 51.
56. *See* White House, President Signs Medicare Legislation, *at* http://www.whitehouse.gov/news/releases/2003/12/print/2003120 8-2.html (Upon signing the bill, President Bush remarked, "Billy

Tauzin of the House of Representatives did great work on this bill") (last visited July 30, 2008).

57. William M. Welch, *Tauzin switches sides from drug industry overseer to lobbyist*, USA TODAY (July 29, 2007), *available at*, http://usatoday.printthis.clickability.com/pt/cpt?action=cpt&title= USATODAY.com (last visited July 30, 2008). Tauzin began negotiations for the position with the Pharmaceutical Research and Manufacturers Association "just a few months after the prescription drug bill passed." CBS NEWS.COM, *supra* note 51.

58. *See* Gregory M. Lamb, *The ABCs of Medicare Part D*, THE CHRISTIAN SCIENCE MONITOR (May 15, 2006), *available at*, http://www.csmonitor.com/2006/0515/p02s02-ussc.htm (last visited July 30, 2008).

59. Statement of David M. Walker, Comptroller General of the United States, "Long-Term fiscal Outlook: Action Is Needed to Avoid the Possibility of a Serious Economic Disruption in the Future," Testimony Before the Committee on the Budget, U.S. Senate (Tuesday, January 29, 2008).

60. *See* CBS NEWS.COM, *supra* note 51.

61. *See* CBS NEWS.COM, *supra* note 51.

62. Robert Pear, *Medicare Official Testifies on Cost Figures*, N.Y. TIMES (March 25, 2004), *available at*, http://query.nytimes.com/gst/fullpage.html?res=9407E4DA1530F 936A15750C0A9629C8 (last visited July 30, 2008).

63. Louis Jacobson and Peter H. Stone, *Former Medicare chief soldiers on in wake of ethics investigations*, NATIONAL JOURNAL (April 9, 2004), *available at*, http://www.govexec.com/dailyfed/0404/040904nj1.htm (last visited July 30, 2008).

64. *See* CBS NEWS.COM, *supra* note 51.

65. *See* CBS NEWS.COM, *supra* note 51.

CHAPTER FOUR

66. *See Former FDA Chief Illegally Held Stocks*, WASHINGTON POST (Tuesday, October 17, 2006) at A19.

67. *See* Marc Kaufman, *Former FDA Chief Joins Lobby Shop*, WASHINGTON POST (Wednesday, February 8, 2006), *available at*, http://www.washingtonpost.com/wp-

dyn/content/article/2006/02/07/AR2006020702693_p (last visited July 30, 2008).
68. *See* Union of Concerned Scientists Summary of Survey Results, *at* http://www.ucsusa.org/news/press_release/fda-scientists-pressured.html (last visited July 30, 2008).
69. *See* National Research Center for Women & Families, *at* http://www.center4research.org/pdf/FDA_Report_9-2006.pdf (last visited July 30, 2008).
70. *See* National Research Center for Women & Families, *supra* note 69.

CHAPTER FIVE

71. Justin Blum, *Whistleblowers Help Congress Strengthen U.S. FDA*, BLOOMBERG.COM (Feb. 8, 2007), *available at*, http://www.bloomberg.com/apps/news?pid=20601103&sid=aDoBKfCg1VfY&refer=news (last visited July 30, 2008).
72. *See Leo Lutwak, 78; Ex-FDA Officer Criticized Its Ties to Drug Companies*, LOS ANGELES TIMES (March 5, 2006), *available at*, http://articles.latimes.com/2006/mar/05/local/me-passings5.4 (last visited July 30, 2008).
73. Keith Addison, *REDUX: Unheeded Warnings on Lethal Diet Pill*, LOS ANGELES TIMES (December 20, 2000), *available at*, http://www.latimes.com/news/nation/reports/fda/lat_redux001220.htm (last visited July 31, 2008).
74. Addison, *supra* note 73.
75. Addison, *supra* note 73.
76. *See* CBS News, *FDA Doc Claims Fen-Phen Cover-Up*, *available at*, http://www.whale.to/v/fen.html (last visited July 31, 2008).
77. *See* Addison, *supra* note 73; Los Angelos Times, *supra* note 72.
78. Addison, *supra* note 73.
79. *See* CBS, "FDA Doc Claims Fen-Phen Cover-Up" at http://www.whale.to/v/fen.html.
80. *See FDA Whistleblower Resigns*, CBS NEWS (October 2, 2000), *available at*, http://www.cbsnews.com/stories/2000/05/05/tech/printable192528.shtml (last visited July 31, 2008).
81. David Willman, *Key Physician Urges Rezulin Be Withdrawn*, LOS ANGELES TIMES (February 19, 2000), *available at*,

http://articles.latimes.com/2000/feb/19/news/n-511; David Willman and Nick Anderson, *Rezulin's Swift Approval, Slow Removal Raise Issues*, LOS ANGELES TIMES (March 23, 2000), *available at*, http://8.12.42.31/2000/mar/23/news/mn-11854.

82. See David Willman, *Physician Who Opposes Rezulin Is Threatened by FDA With Dismissal* (March 17, 2000), at http://www.pulitzer.org/year/2001/investigative-reporting/works/willman5.html.
83. See Willman, *supra* note 82.
84. David Willman, *Risk Was Known as FDA OKd Fatal Drug*, LOS ANGELES TIMES (March 11, 2001), *available at*, http://articles.latimes.com/2001/mar/11/news/mn-36273 (last visited July 31, 2008).
85. Willman, *Risk was Known*, *supra* note 84.
86. Willman, *Key Physician Urges*, *supra* note 81.
87. Willman, *Key Physician Urges*, *supra* note 81.
88. Willman, *Key Physician Urges*, *supra* note 81.
89. David Willman and Nick Anderson, *Rezulin's Swift Approval, Slow Removal Raise Issues*, LOS ANGELES TIMES (March 23, 2000), *available at*, http://8.12.42.31/2000/mar/23/news/mn-11854 (last visited July 31, 2008).
90. Willman, *Key Physician Urges*, *supra* note 81.
91. Willman, *Key Physician Urges*, *supra* note 81.
92. *Diabetes drug Rezulin taken off market*, CNN.COM (march 23, 2000), *at*, http://archives.cnn.com/2000/HEALTH/03/22/diabetes.drug.01/ (last visited July 31, 2008).
93. Michael Scherer, *The Side Effects of Truth*, MOTHER JONES (May 1, 2005), *at*, http://www.motherjones.com/news/feature/2005/05/david_graham.html (last visited July 31, 2008).
94. CBS News, *Whistle Blower Resigns*, *supra* note 80.
95. *Another FDA Whistleblower Speaks*, CBS NEWS (March 20, 2000), *at*, http:www.cbsnews.com/stories/2000/03/20/national/printable174255.shtml (last visited July 31, 2008); Willman, *Risk was Known*, *supra* note 84.
96. Willman, *Risk was Known*, *supra* note 84; CNN.com, *Rezulin taken off market*, *supra* note 92.
97. Willman & Anderson, *Rezulin's Swift Approval*, *supra* note 89.

98. Quoted in Evelyn Pringle, *FDA Scientist Graham Calls Glaxo Avandia Trial Useless*, LAWYERSANDSETTLEMENTS.COM (July 30, 2007), *at*, http://www.lawyersandsettlements.com/articles/01198/avandia-online-study.html (last visited July 31, 2008).
99. Kim Dixon, *FDA staffer seeks higher standards after Avandia concerns*, REUTERS HEALTH (Nov. 27, 2007), *available at*, http://www.rtmagazine.com/reuters_article.asp?mode=print&id=2 0071127rglt005.html (last visited July 31, 2008).
100. Gardiner Harris, *Report Backs Up Warnings About Drug Avandia*, N. Y. TIMES (July 27, 2007), *available at*, http://www.nytimes.com/2007/07/27/health/27avandia.html?ref=h ealth&pagewanted=print (last visited July 31, 2008).
101. Gardiner Harris, *F.D.A. Issues Strictest Warning on Diabetes Drugs*, N.Y. TIMES (June 7, 2007), *available at*, http://www.nytimes.com/2007/06/07/health/07drug.html (last visited July 31, 2008).
102. Gardiner Harris, *Potentially Incompatible Goals at F.D.A.*, N.Y. TIMES (June 11, 2007), *available at*, http://www.nytimes.com/2007/06/11/washington/11fda.html?page warnted=print (last visited July 31, 2008).
103. Dixon, *supra* note 99; Ramsey Baghda, *Avandia and the Commercial Impact of FDA's Credibility Gap*, 2 (9) THE RPM REPORT, *available at*, http://therpmreport.com/EMS_Base/Agent.aspx?Page=/Content/2 007500150.aspx (last visited July 31, 2008).
104. *See* Harris, *Diabetes Drugs*, *supra* note 101.
105. Gardiner Harris, *Potentially Incompatible Goals at F.D.A.*, N.Y. TIMES (June 11, 2007), *available at,* http://www.nytimes.com/2007/06/11/washington/11fda.html?page wanted=print (last visited July 31, 2008).
106. Baghda, *Credibility Gap*, *supra* note 103.
107. *See* "Testimony of David J. Graham, MD, MPH, November 18, 2004," before the Senate Finance Committee.
108. *See* Scherer, *Side Effects of Truth*, *supra* note 93.
109. *See* Scherer, *Side Effects of Truth*, *supra* note 93.
110. "Testimony of David J. Graham, MD, MPH, November 18, 2004."
111. "Testimony of David J. Graham, MD, MPH, November 18, 2004."
112. Gardiner Harris, *F.D.A. Failing in Drug Safety, Official Asserts*, N.Y. TIMES (November 19, 2004), *available at*,

http://www.nytimes.com/2004/11/19/business/19fda.html (last visited July 31, 2008).
113. "Testimony of David J. Graham, MD, MPH, November 18, 2004."
114. Dick Carozza, *An Interview with Dr. David J. Graham, Associate Director of the FDA's Office of Drug Safety*, FRAUD MAGAZINE (September/October 2005) at 41.
115. Carozza, *supra* note 114.
116. Quoted in Dick Carozza, *supra* note 114, at 37.
117. "Testimony of David J. Graham, MD, MPH, November 18, 2004."
118. Marc Kaufman, *Whistle-Blower Guardians Say FDA Officials Tried to Undermine Critic*, SAN FRANCISCO CHRONICLE (November 24, 2004), *available at*, http://www.commondreams.org/headlines04/1124-04.htm (July 31, 2008).
119. *See* Donna Young, *Whistleblowers Tell Congress of Ketek Problems*, American Society of Health-System Pharmacists, HEALTHY-SYSTEM PHARMACY NEWS, *available at*, http://www.ashp.org/s_ashp/article_news.asp?CID=167&DID=2024&id=18701 (last visited July 31, 2008).
120. Blum, *Whistleblowers help Congress*, *supra* note 71.
121. *See* Young, *supra* note 119.
122. *See* Young, *supra* note 119.
123. *See* Young, *supra* note 119.
124. David B. Ross, *The FDA and the Case of Ketek*, 356 (16) NEW ENG. J. OF MED. 1601-02 (April 19, 2007).
125. Tom Lamb, *Allegation by FDA Whistleblower David Ross Adds to Controversy over Antibiotic Ketek; Former FDA Scientist Claims Agency Superiors Downplayed His Pre-approval Concerns About Safety of Ketek*, DRUG INJURY WATCH, *at*, http://www.drug-injury.com/druginjurycom/2007/02/allegations_by_.html (last visited July 31, 2008).
126. Norman M. Goldfarb, *David Ross on the FDA*, 3 (11) JOURNAL OF CLINICAL RESEARCH BEST PRACTICES (November 2007).
127. Ross, *supra* note 124.
128. Kris Hundley, *Drug's chilling path to market: How a broken FDA approved a cold antibiotic despite a wide trail of alarms*, TAMPA-BAY.COM (May 27, 2007), *at*, http://www.sptimes.com/2007/05/27/news_pf/Worldandnation/Drug_s_chilling__path.shtml (last visited July 31, 2008).
129. Norman M. Goldfarb, *David Ross on the FDA*, 3 (11) JOURNAL OF CLINICAL RESEARCH BEST PRACTICES (November 2007).

130. Goldfarb, *supra* note 129.
131. Ross, *supra* note 124.
132. Goldfarb, *supra* note 129.
133. Joanne Silberner, *FDA to Leave Antibiotic Ketek on the Market*, NPR (July 17, 2008), *at*, http://www.npr.org/templates/story/story.php?storyId=6635165 (last visited July 31, 2008); Rita Rubin, *Vioxx whistle-blower weighs in on demoted antibiotic Ketek*, USA TODAY (February 13, 2007), *at*, http://www.usatoday.com/news/health/2007-02-13-fda-oversight_x.htm (last visited July 31, 2008).
134. Kris Hundley, *Drug's chilling path to market: How a broken FDa approved a cold antibiotic despite a wide trail of alarms*, TAMPA-BAY.COM (May 27, 2007) at http://www.sptimes.com/2007/05/27/news_pf/Worldandnation/Drug_s_chilling__path.shtml (last visited July 31, 2008).
135. *See McMan's Depression and Bipolar Web* at http://www.mcmanweb.com/FDA_suicide.htm (last visited July 31, 2008).
136. Benedict Carey, *Youth, meds and suicide*, LOS ANGELES TIMES (February 2, 2004), *at*, http://articles.latimes.com/2004/feb/02/health/he-ssri2 (last visited July 31, 2008).
137. *See* Gardiner Harris, *Antidepressant Study Seen to Back Expert*, N.Y. TIMES (August 20, 2004), *at*, http://query.nytimes.com/gst/fullpage.html?res=9D01E5D61F3FF933A1575BC0A9629C8B63 (last visited July 31, 2008).
138. *See* Jeanne Lenzer, *Secret US report survaces on antidepressants in children*, BRITISH MEDICAL JOURNAL (August 7, 2004), *at*, http://bmj.bmjjournals.com/cgi/content/full/329/7461/307 (last visited July 31, 2008).
139. *See McMan's Depression and Bipolar Web*, *at*, http://www.mcmanweb.com/FDA_suicide.htm (last visited July 31, 2008).
140. *See* Lenzer, *supra* note 138.
141. *See* Gardiner Harris, *Potentially Incompatible Goals at F.D.A.*, N.Y. TIMES (June 11, 2007) at http://www.nytimes.com/2007/06/11/washington/11fda.html?pagewanted=print (last visited July 31, 2008).
142. *Antidepressant Danger for Kids?* CBSNEWS.COM (February 2, 2004), *at*

http://www.cbsnews.com/stories/2004/02/02/health/printable5973 31.shtml (last visited July 31, 2008).
143. CBSNews.com, *supra* note 142; Bruce Levine, *Corporate Fraud Behind the Paxil Scandals*, Z MAGAZINE (reprinted by The International Center for the Study of Psychiatry and Psychology), *available at*, http://www.icspp.org?World-Opinion/corporate-Fraud-Behind-the-Paxil-Scandals.html (last visited July 31, 2008).
144. Kelly Patricia O'Meara, *Will British Ban Spur FDA to Act?* PSYCHDRUGTRUTH, *at*, http://www.prozactruth.com/article_british_ban_spur_fda.htm (last visited July 31, 2008).
145. Carozza, *Interview with Dr. David J. Graham*, *supra* note 114.
146. *See* Harris, *Antidepressant Study*, *supra* note 137; Elizabeth Shogren, *FDA Sat On Report Linking Suicide, Drugs*, LOS ANGELES TIMES (April 6, 2004), *at*, http://articles.latimes.com/2004/apr/06/nation/na-suicide6 (last visited July 31, 2008).
147. "Testimony of David J. Graham, MD, MPH, November 18, 2004"; Carozza, *Interview with Dr. David J. Graham*, *supra* note 114.
148. "Testimony of David J. Graham, MD, MPH, November 18, 2004."
149. Carozza, *Interview with Dr. David J. Graham*, *supra* note 114, at 40.
150. Evelyn Pringle, *FDA Hounded Over Ketek Scandal*, LAWYERSANDSETTLEMENTS.COM (March 19, 2007), *at*, http://www.lawyersandsettlements.com/articles/00680/ketek-scandal.html (last visited July 31, 2008).
151. Kris Hundley, *Drug's chilling path to market: How a broken FDa approved a cold antibiotic despite a wide trail of alarms*, TAMPABAY.COM (May 27, 2007), *at*, http://www.sptimes.com/2007/05/27/news_pf/Worldandnation/Drug_s_chilling__path.shtml (July 31, 2008).
152. Carozza, *Interview with Dr. David J. Graham*, *supra* note 114, at 39.

CHAPTER SIX

153. 502 U.S. 577, 626 (1992) (Souter, J. concurring).
154. 164 F.3d 650, 653 (D.C. Cir. 1999).
155. *See* Pearson v. Shalala, 14 F.Supp.2d 10 (D.D.C. 1998).

156. 164 F.3d 650 (D.C. Cir. 1999).
157. 172 F.3d at 655.
158. 172 F.3d at 657.
159. 172 F.3d at 661.
160. *See* Pearson v. Shalala, 172 F.3d 72 (D.C. Cir. 1999).
161. *See* Pearson v. Shalala II, 130 F.Supp.2d 105 (D.D.C. 2001); 65 Fed. Reg. 58917, 58918 (Oct. 3, 2000).
162. Pearson v. Shalala II, 130 F.Supp.2d 105, 117 (D.D.C. 2001).
163. Pearson v. Shalala II, 130 F.Supp.2d 105, 117 (D.D.C. 2001).
164. Pearson v. Shalala II, 130 F.Supp.2d 105, 117 (D.D.C. 2001).
165. Pearson v. Shalala II, 130 F.Supp.2d 105, 112, 118-119, 120 (D.D.C. 2001).
166. Pearson v. Shalala III, 141 F.Supp.2d 105, 112 (D.D.C. 2001).
167. Whitaker v. Thompson I, 284 F.Supp.2d 1 (D.D.C. 2002).
168. Whitaker v. Thompson I, 284 F.Supp.2d 1, 13, 15 (D.D.C. 2002).
169. Rule *Food Labeling; Health Messages and Label Statements; Reproposed Rule*, 55 Fed. Reg. 5176, 5192 (1990). Congressional awareness of FDA's preferred definition is apparent from the legislative record. *See* "Nutrition Labeling and Education Act of 1990," House Report 101-538 at 21.
170. *See Labeling; General Requirements for Health Claims for Food*, 56 Fed. Reg. 60537, 60542 (1991); 21 C.F.R. § 101.14(a)(1).
171. *See* NLEA, House Report 101-538, 101st Cong., 2nd Sess. (June 13, 1990) at 9: ". . . [D]uring the mid-1980s, companies began making *health claims* on foods, even though the FDA had not approved the claims through the drug approval process. These statements claimed that the food was valuable in the *prevention or treatment of various diseases*" and ". . . there is a serious question as to whether the Agency has the legal authority to implement the program that it has proposed, *which would permit health claims regarding the usefulness of a food in treating a disease . . .*"
172. Among the direct treatment associations the Committee understood the NLEA health claims provision would embrace are those for garlic reducing serum blood cholesterol (S. Rep. 103-410 at 11); ginger relieving nausea and stomach distress (S. Rep. 103-410 at 11); the bioflavonoid quercitin reducing the allergy-inflammatory response (S. Rep. 103-410 at 14); and glucosamine sulfate repairing damaged joints (S. Rep. 103-410 at 14).
173. Whitaker v. Thompson, 239 F.Supp.2d 43 (D.D.C. 2003).
174. Whitaker v. Thompson III, 353 F.3d 947 (D.C. Cir. 2004).

175. *See* 21 USC 343(r); 21 CFR 101.93; "Regulations on Statements Made for Dietary Supplements Concerning the Effect of the Product on the Structure or Function of the Body; Final Rule," 65 Fed. Reg. 1000 (Jan. 6, 2000).
176. National Institute of Arthritis and Musculoskeletal and Skin Diseases at http://www.webmd.com/osteoarthritis/guide/national-institute-arthritis-musculoskeletal-skin-diseases.
177. Letter to Jonathan W. Emord, dated October 12, 2004, from Michael M. Landa, Director of Regulatory Affairs, Center for Food Safety and Applied Nutrition.
178. *See* "Alli Side Effects" at http://www.allipills.com/weight-loss-pills/alli-side-effects.html.

CHAPTER SEVEN

179. *See* 21 U.S.C. § 321(g)(1)(B) (2008).
180. 21 U.S.C. §§ 331(d), 355(a).
181. Sheryl Gay Stolberg, *F.D.A. Officials Press Legislators to Oppose Bill on Importing Less Expensive Drugs*, N.Y. TIMES (Jul. 25, 2003), *available at*, http://query.nytimes.com/gst/fullpage.html?res=9B04EFD7123FF936A15754C0A9659C8B63&sec=&spon=&pagewanted=1 (last visited August 1, 2008).
182. 21 U.S.C. §§ 321(p), 332, 334.
183. *See Methamphetamine: Preventing the Retail Diversion of Pseudoephedrine, at*, http://www.deadiversion.usdoj.gov/pubs/brochures/pseudo/pseudo_trifold.htm (last visited July 31, 2008).
184. *See, e.g., Mexico Meth Floods U.S., at*, http://www.cbsnews.com/stories/2006/05/19/eveningnews/main1636846.shtml (last visited July 31, 2008).
185. See, e.g., MB Wholesale, Inc.; Denial of Application, 72 FR 71956 (Dec. 19, 2007); Ammar Sabbagh; Denial of Application, 72 FR 68196 (Dec. 4, 2007); Tim's Wholesale; Denial of Application, 72 FR 58890 (Oct. 17, 2007); Archer's Trading Company; Revocation of Registration, 72 F.R. 42114 (Aug. 1, 2007); Holloway Distributing; Revocation of Registration, 72 F.R. 42118 (Aug. 2007); John J. Fotinopoulos; Revocation of Registration, 72 FR 24602 (May 3, 2007); Rick's Picks, L.L.C.; Revocation of Registration, 72 FR 18275 (Apr. 11, 2007); Planet

Trading, Inc., d/b/a/ United Wholesale Distributors, Inc.; Denial of Application, 72 FR 11055 (Mar. 12, 2007); ATF Fitness Products, Inc.; Denial of Application, Tuesday, 72 FR 9967 (Mar. 6, 2007); Georgia Convenience Wholesale, Inc.; Denial of Application, 72 FR 9969 (Mar. 6, 2007); MK Distributing, Inc.; Denial of Application, 72 FR 9972 (Mar. 6, 2007); Stephen J. Heldman, Denial Of Application, 72 FR 4032 (Jan. 29, 2007); Wild West Wholesale; Revocation of Registration, Monday, 72 FR 4042 (Jan. 29, 2007); Taby Enterprises of Osceola, Inc.; Denial of Application, 71 FR 71557 (Dec. 11, 2006); T. Young Associates, Inc.; Revocation of Registration; Introduction and Procedural History, 71 FR 60567 (Oct. 13, 2006); Gregg Brothers Wholesale Co., Inc.; Denial of Application, 71 FR 59830 (Oct. 11, 2006); Premier Holdings, Inc.; Denial of Application, 71 FR 59834 (Oct. 11, 2006); Nashville Wholesale Company, Inc.; Denial of Application, 71 FR 52159 (Sept. 1, 2006); Tri-County Bait Distributors; Denial of Application, 71 FR 52160 (Sept. 1, 2006); Sujak Distributors; Denial of Application, 71 FR 50102 (Aug. 24, 2006); John Vanags; Denial of Application, 71 FR 39365 (July 12, 2006); David M. Starr; Denial of Application, 71 FR 39367 (July 12, 2006); D & S Sales, Revocation of Registration; Introduction and Procedural History, 71 FR 37607 (June 30, 2006); McBride Marketing; Revocation of Registration, 71 FR 35710 (June 21, 2006); H & R Corporation; Denial of Application, 71 FR 30168 (May 25, 2006); Joey Enterprises, Inc. d/b/a/ NorthStar Wholesale; Denial of Application, 70 FR 76866 (Dec. 28, 2005); Joy's Ideas, Revocation of Registration, 70 FR 33195 (Jun. 7, 2005); A-1 Distribution Wholesale; Denial of Registration, 70 FR 28573 (May 18, 2005); ELK International, Inc., d.b.a. Tri-City Wholesale; Denial of Application, Tuesday70 FR 24615 (May 10, 2005); Jay Enterprises of Spartanburg, Inc.; Denial of Registration, 70 FR 24620 (May 10, 2005); Net Wholesale; Revocation of Registration, 70 FR 24626 (May 10, 2005); Titan Wholesale, Inc.; Denial of Registration, 70 FR 12727 (Mar. 15, 2005); TNT Distributors, Inc., Denial of Application, 70 FR 12729 (Mar. 15, 2005); Tysa Management, d/b/a Osmani Lucky Wholesale; Denial of Application, 70 FR 12732 (March 15, 2005); RAM, INC. d/b/a American Wholesale Distribution Corp.; Denial of Registration, 70 FR 11693 (March 9, 2005); Al-Alousi, Inc., Denial of Registration, 70 FR 3561 (January 25, 2005); CWK Enterprises, Inc.; Denial of Registration, 69 FR 69400 (Nov. 29,

2004); Prachi Enterprises, Inc.; Denial of Registration, 69 FR 69407 (Nov. 29, 2004); Volusia Wholesale; Denial of Registration, 69 FR 69409 (Nov. 29, 2004); Absolute Distributing, Inc.; Denial of Registration, 69 FR 62078 (October 22, 2004); Express Wholesale Denial of Application, 69 FR 62086 (Oct. 22, 2004); J & S Distributors; Denial of Application, 69 FR 62089 (Oct. 22, 2004); Value Wholesale Denial of Registration, 69 FR 58548 (Sept. 30, 2004); K & Z Enterprises, Inc.; Denial of Application, 69 FR 51475 August 19, 2004; John E. McCrae d/b/a J & H Wholesale; Denial of Application, 69 FR 51480 (August 19, 2004); Proveedora Jiron, Inc. Edilberto Jiron, President; Denial of Application, 69 FR 51481 (Aug. 19, 2004);William E. "Bill" Smith d/b/a B & B Wholesale; Denial of Application, 69 FR 22559 (Apr. 26, 2004); Gazaly Trading; Denial of Application, 69 FR 22561 (Apr. 26, 2004); ANM Wholesale; Denial of Application, 69 FR 11652 (Mar. 11, 2004); Direct Wholesale Denial of Application, 69 FR 11654 (Mar. 11, 2004); Branex, Incorporated; Revocation of Registration, 69 FR 8682 (Feb. 25, 2004); Shop It For Profit; Denial of Application, 69 FR 1311 (Jan. 8, 2004).

186. *See, e.g., Sinbad Distributing; Denial of Application*, 67 Fed. Reg. 10232 (Mar. 6, 2002).

CHAPTER EIGHT

187. Jonathan W. Emord, *Murder by Medicare: The Demise of Solo and Small Group Medical Practices*, 21 (3) REGULATION 31-39 (1998).
188. *See* 42 C.F.R § 405.904(a)(2).

CHAPTER NINE

189. Montesquieu, *The Spirit of the Laws* 121 (ed. by Cohler, Miller & Stone) (Cambridge University Press, 2000).
190. 467 U.S. 837, 842-843 (1984).
191. 467 U.S. 837, 843-844 (1984).

EPILOGUE

192. Ronald Wilson Reagan, First Inaugural Address, January 20, 1981.

BIBLIOGRAPHY

1. John Abramson, *Overdosed America* (Harper Collins, 2004).

2. John Adams, *Thoughts on Government*, in THE PAPERS OF JOHN ADAMS 4:86-93 (Robert J. Taylor et al. eds., Belknap Press, Harvard University Press, 1977) (1776).

3. Keith Addison, *REDUX: Unheeded Warnings on Lethal Diet Pill*, LOS ANGELES TIMES (December 20, 2000), *available at*, http://www.latimes.com/news/nation/reports/fda/lat_redux001220.htm (last visited July 31, 2008).

4. Marcia Angell, *The Truth About the Drug Companies* 142 (Random House, 2004).

5. Ramsey Baghda, *Avandia and the Commercial Impact of FDA's Credibility Gap*, 2 (9) THE RPM REPORT, *available at*, http://therpmreport.com/EMS_Base/Agent.aspx?Page=/Content/2007500150.aspx (last visited July 31, 2008).

6. Bernard Bailyn, *The Ideological Origins of the American Revolution* 36 (Belknap Press, Harvard University Press, 1967)

7. Leonard Baker, *Back to Back: The Duel between FDR and the Supreme Court* (New York: Macmillan, 1967).

8. Justin Blum, *Whistleblowers Help Congress Strengthen U.S. FDA*, BLOOMBERG.COM (Feb. 8, 2007), *available at*, http://www.bloomberg.com/apps/news?pid=20601103&sid=aDoBKfCg1VfY&refer=news (last visited July 30, 2008).

9. Bolingbroke in VI *Craftsman* No. 198 (London, 1731).

10. Benedict Carey, *Youth, meds and suicide*, LOS ANGELES TIMES (February 2, 2004), *at*, http://articles.latimes.com/2004/feb/02/health/he-ssri2 (last visited July 31, 2008).

11. Dick Carozza, *An Interview with Dr. David J. Graham, Associate Director of the FDA's Office of Drug Safety*, FRAUD MAGAZINE (September/October 2005).

12. Kim Dixon, *FDA staffer seeks higher standards after Avandia concerns*, REUTERS HEALTH (Nov. 27, 2007), *available at*, http://www.rtmagazine.com/reuters_article.asp?mode=print&id=2007 1127rglt005.html (last visited July 31, 2008).

13. Jonathan W. Emord, *Murder by Medicare: The Demise of Solo and Small Group Medical Practices*, 21 (3) REGULATION 31-39 (1998).

14. Ian Fleming, *You Only Live Twice* (1964).

15. Douglas H. Ginsburg, "Delegation Running Riot," a review of *Power Without Responsibility: How Congress Abuses the People through Delegation* by David Schoenbrod, REGULATION (1995), *available at*, www.cato.org/pubs/regulation/reg18n1f.html.

16. Norman M. Goldfarb, *David Ross on the FDA*, 3 (11) JOURNAL OF CLINICAL RESEARCH BEST PRACTICES (November 2007).

17. Steve Goldstein, "U.S. prescription drug sales growth slowed to 3.8% in 2007," WALL ST. J. DIGITAL WATCH, (MarketWatch, March 12, 2008), *at* http://www.marketwatch.com/news/story/us-prescription-drug-sales-growth/story.aspx?guid=%7B37AD0634-681C-4E1A-AC1F-E364D027B3C9%7D (last visited July 30, 2008).

18. Gardiner Harris, *Report Backs Up Warnings About Drug Avandia*, N.Y. TIMES (July 27, 2007), *available at*, http://www.nytimes.com/2007/07/27/health/27avandia.html?ref=healt h&pagewanted=print (last visited July 31, 2008).

19. Gardiner Harris, *F.D.A. Issues Strictest Warning on Diabetes Drugs*, N.Y. TIMES (June 7, 2007), *available at*, http://www.nytimes.com/2007/06/07/health/07drug.html (last visited July 31, 2008).

20. Gardiner Harris, *Potentially Incompatible Goals at F.D.A.*, N.Y. TIMES (June 11, 2007), *available at*, http://www.nytimes.com/2007/06/11/washington/11fda.html?pagewa nted=print (last visited July 31, 2008).

21. Gardiner Harris, *F.D.A. Failing in Drug Safety, Official Asserts*, N.Y. TIMES (November 19, 2004), *available at*, http://www.nytimes.com/2004/11/19/business/19fda.html (last visited July 31, 2008).

22. Gardiner Harris, *Antidepressant Study Seen to Back Expert*, N.Y. TIMES (August 20, 2004), *at*, http://query.nytimes.com/gst/fullpage.html?res=9D01E5D61F3FF933 A1575BC0A9629C8B63 (last visited July 31, 2008).

23. Kris Hundley, *Drug's chilling path to market: How a broken FDA approved a cold antibiotic despite a wide trail of alarms*, TAMPA-BAY.COM (May 27, 2007), *at*, http://www.sptimes.com/2007/05/27/news_pf/Worldandnation/Drug_s_chilling__path.shtml (last visited July 31, 2008).

24. Sanford Ikeda, "Rent-Seeking: A Primer," 53 (11) *The Freeman* (Nov. 2003).

25. Louis Jacobson and Peter H. Stone, *Former Medicare chief soldiers on in wake of ethics investigations*, NATIONAL JOURNAL (April 9, 2004), *available at*, http://www.govexec.com/dailyfed/0404/040904nj1.htm (last visited July 30, 2008).

26. Thomas Jefferson, *Kentucky Resolutions* (1798).

27. Thomas Jefferson, *Notes on the State of Virginia*, Query 13, 120-121 (1784).

28. Marc Kaufman, *Former FDA Chief Joins Lobby Shop*, WASHINGTON POST (Wednesday, February 8, 2006), *available at*, http://www.washingtonpost.com/wp-dyn/content/article/2006/02/07/AR2006020702693_p (last visited July 30, 2008).

29. Marc Kaufman, *Whistle-Blower Guardians Say FDA Officials Tried to Undermine Critic*, SAN FRANCISCO CHRONICLE (November 24, 2004), *available at*, http://www.commondreams.org/headlines04/1124-04.htm (July 31, 2008).

30. Gregory M. Lamb, *The ABCs of Medicare Part D*, THE CHRISTIAN SCIENCE MONITOR (May 15, 2006), *available at*, http://www.csmonitor.com/2006/0515/p02s02-ussc.htm (last visited July 30, 2008).

31. Tom Lamb, *Allegation by FDA Whistleblower David Ross Adds to Controversy over Antibiotic Ketek; Former FDA Scientist Claims*

Agency Superiors Downplayed His Pre-approval Concerns About Safety of Ketek, DRUG INJURY WATCH, *at*, http://www.drug-injury.com/druginjurycom/2007/02/allegations_by_.html (last visited July 31, 2008).

32. Jeanne Lenzer, *Secret US report surfaces on antidepressants in children*, BRITISH MEDICAL JOURNAL (August 7, 2004), *at*, http://bmj.bmjjournals.com/cgi/content/full/329/7461/307 (last visited July 31, 2008).

33. Bruce Levine, *Corporate Fraud Behind the Paxil Scandals*, Z MAGAZINE (reprinted by The International Center for the Study of Psychiatry and Psychology), *available at*, http://www.icspp.org?WorldOpinion/corporate-Fraud-Behind-the-Paxil-Scandals.html (last visited July 31, 2008).

34. William Leuchtenburg, *The Origins of Franklin D. Roosevelt's 'Court-Packing Plan,'* SUPREME COURT REVIEW 347-400 (1966).

35. David E. Lewis, *Presidents and the Politics of Agency Design: Political Insulation in the United States Government Bureaucracy, 1946-1997* at 42-44 (Stanford University Press, 2003).

36. John Locke, *Two Treatises of Government* 2d Treatise, (Peter Laslett ed., Mentor Books 1965) (1689)

37. *Leo Lutwak, 78; Ex-FDA Officer Criticized Its Ties to Drug Companies*, LOS ANGELES TIMES (March 5, 2006), *available at*, http://articles.latimes.com/2006/mar/05/local/me-passings5.4 (last visited July 30, 2008).

38. THE FEDERALIST NO. 47, at 303 (James Madison, Alexander Hamilton, & John Jay) (Isaac Kramnick ed., Penguin Books 1987).

39. Montesquieu, *The Spirit of the Laws* 157 (Cohler, Miller & Stone eds., Cambridge University Press 2000).

40. National Institute for Health Care Management Foundation, *Prescription Drugs and Intellectual Property Protection: Finding the Right Balance Between Access and Innovation* at 10 (2000).

41. Kelly Patricia O'Meara, *Will British Ban Spur FDA to Act?* PSYCHDRUGTRUTH, *at*,

http://www.prozactruth.com/article_british_ban_spur_fda.htm (last visited July 31, 2008).

42. Evelyn Pringle, *FDA Scientist Graham Calls Glaxo Avandia Trial Useless*, LAWYERSANDSETTLEMENTS.COM (July 30, 2007), *at*, http://www.lawyersandsettlements.com/articles/01198/avandia-online-study.html (last visited July 31, 2008).

43. Evelyn Pringle, *FDA Hounded Over Ketek Scandal*, LAWYERSAND-SETTLEMENTS.COM (March 19, 2007), *at*, http://www.lawyersandsettlements.com/articles/00680/ketek-scandal.html (last visited July 31, 2008).

44. David B. Ross, *The FDA and the Case of Ketek*, 356 (16) NEW ENG. J. OF MED. 1601-02 (April 19, 2007).

45. Rita Rubin, *Vioxx whistle-blower weighs in on demoted antibiotic Ketek*, USA TODAY (February 13, 2007), *at*, http://www.usatoday.com/news/health/2007-02-13-fda-oversight_x.htm (last visited July 31, 2008).

46. David Schoenbrod, *Power Without Responsibility: How Congress Abuses the People Through Delegation* 10 (Yale University Press, 1993).

47. Bernard H. Siegan, *Economic Liberties and the Constitution* 3-4 (University of Chicago Press, 1980).

48. Joanne Silberner, *FDA to Leave Antibiotic Ketek on the Market*, NPR (July 17, 2008), *at*, http://www.npr.org/templates/story/story.php?storyId=6635165 (last visited July 31, 2008).

49. George J. Stigler, *The theory of economic regulation*, BELL J. ECON. MAN. SCI. 2:3-21 (1971).

50. Nicholas J. Szabo, *Origins of the Non-Delegation Doctrine*, Seminar Paper, the George Washington University Law School, at 15, *available at*, http://szabo.best.vwh.net/delegation.pdf.

51. Gordon Tullock, *The Welfare Costs of Tariffs, Monopolies, and Theft*, 5 W. ECON. J. 224-232 (1967).

52. David Willman, *Key Physician Urges Rezulin Be Withdrawn*, LOS ANGELES TIMES (February 19, 2000), *available at*, http://articles.latimes.com/2000/feb/19/news/n-511.

53. David Willman, *Physician Who Opposes Rezulin Is Threatened by FDA With Dismissal* (March 17, 2000), at http://www.pulitzer.org/year/2001/investigative-reporting/works/willman5.html.

54. David Willman, *Risk Was Known as FDA OKd Fatal Drug*, LOS ANGELES TIMES (March 11, 2001), *available at*, http://articles.latimes.com/2001/mar/11/news/mn-36273 (last visited July 31, 2008).

55. David Willman and Nick Anderson, *Rezulin's Swift Approval, Slow Removal Raise Issues*, LOS ANGELES TIMES (March 23, 2000), *available at*, http://8.12.42.31/2000/mar/23/news/mn-11854.

56. Alastair J.J. Wood, "A Proposal for Radical Changes in the Drug-Approval Process," 355 NEW ENG. J. MED. 618 (Aug. 10, 2006).

57. Donna Young, *Whistleblowers Tell Congress of Ketek Problems*, American Society of Health-System Pharmacists, HEALTHY-SYSTEM PHARMACY NEWS, *available at*, http://www.ashp.org/s_ashp/article_news.asp?CID=167&DID=2024&id=18701 (last visited July 31, 2008).

58. 1 THE FOUNDERS' CONSTITUTION 443 (Philip B. Kurland and Ralph Lerner eds.) (1987).

59. THE FEDERALIST NO. 4 (James Madison, Alexander Hamilton, & John Jay).

INDEX

Abuse of Power, 10-11, 14-20, 27-28, 40-46, 66, 90, 103-122
Alexander Hamilton, 15, 123, 124, 125, 145, 147
Alien and Sedition Acts, 68
Andrew D. Mosholder, 62-64
Andrew von Eschenbach, 53
Anne Krueger, 31
Antioxidant vitamins, 72, 79-81
Avandia, 52–53, 52, 53, 132, 133, 141, 142, 145
Benign prostatic hyperplasia, 83
Billy Tauzin, 35-38
Bureaucratic Oligarchy, 11
Cancer, 72, 79, 83
Censorship, 68-85, 114-117
Centers for Medicare and Medicaid Services, 8, 37, 40, 41, 46
Center for Drug Evaluation and Research, 47, 49, 54
Center for Food Safety and Applied Nutrition, 81
Charles de Secondat de Montesquieu, 14, 15, 16, 102, 124, 125, 139, 145
Chevron doctrine, 19, 20, 83, 109
Chondroitin sulfate, 86-87
Collocation of Powers, 9–13, 21-22
  CMS, 40–42
  DEA, 40–42
  FDA, 40–42
Commodity Futures Trading Commission, 8
Conflicts of interest, 44
Constitution-in-exile, 26
Consumer Product Safety Commission, 8, 27
Coronary heart disease, 72,
Dan Burton, 33, 36
David J. Graham, 50, 53-59, 62, 64, 65, 66, 108
David Kessler, 71-72
David B. Ross, 59-62
David M. Walker, 35-36
Drug defined, 68, 83
Delegation, 21–24
Drug Enforcement Administration, 8, 40, 45, 93
  anti-competitive actions, 91–94
  diversion, 93
Drug monopoly, 32-39, 91-94
Durk Pearson, 71-82
Effexor, 62–65, 62
Federal Communications Commission, 1, 2, 8, 103
  Mark Fowler, 2
Federal Trade Commission, 8, 104
Fiber, 72
Food and Drug Administration, 11, 4, 5, 8, 32, 33, 39, 40, 41, 42, 43, 44, 45, 47, 48, 49, 50, 51, 52, 53, 54, 55, 56, 57, 58,

59, 60, 61, 62, 63, 64, 65, 66, 68, 69, 70, 71, 72, 73, 74, 75, 76, 77, 78, 79, 80, 81, 82, 83, 84, 90, 91, 92, 103, 104, 107, 108, 111, 112, 113, 114-117, 130, 131, 132, 133, 134, 135, 136, 137, 138, 141, 142, 143, 144, 145, 146
FDA Advisory Committees, 44-45
anti-competitive actions, 91–94
intended use doctrine, 70
new drug approval process, 32, 56, 69, 71, 91
refusal to implement constitutional mandates, 75, 76, 78, 82
third party literature, 92
whistleblowers, 42
FDA health claim redefinition, 82-83
FDA letters to Jonathan Emord, 79, 83
Folic acid, 114
Founders' view on power, 105
Francesca Grifo, 66
Franklin Delano Roosevelt, 24, 25, 126, 144
court packing plan, 25
New Deal, 24, 25, 27, 126
new deal cases, 24–25
George H. W. Bush, 3
reregulation, 4
George J. Stigler, 30, 127, 146
industry capture, 30
George W. Bush, 4
lack of presidential leadership, 4
ambivalence to deregulation, 4
reregulation, 4
George Washington, 9, 15, 18, 112, 120, 141
GordonTullock, 29, 31-32, 127, 148
GlaxoSmithKline, 52, 89
Glucosamine, 86, 87
Health Claim defined, 79
Health Claims, 68-73, 77-78, 82-87
Health Insurance Portability and Accountability Act, 97
Industry capture, 30-39, 102-103
James Madison, 11, 14, 15, 16, 17, 68, 123, 124, 125, 145, 147
John Adams, 15, 124, 141
John Locke, 23, 124, 144
John Powers, 60
John Trenchard, 17
Jonathan W. Emord, 1-7
Campaign for Reagan, 1
Constitution in peril, 6-7, 12-13
First Amendment seminar, 1
Reaganite, 2-3
FCC, 2
John Abramson, 5
George H.W. Bush, 3-4
George W. Bush, 3-4
Mark Fowler, 2
Dennis Patrick, 2

INDEX

Ron Paul, 5
Ronald Reagan, 1-3, 5
Kent Snyder, 5
Durk Pearson and Sandy Shaw, 71-82
Pearson ligitation, 68-69, 71-79, 81-83
Whitaker litigation, 75, 79-84, 88-89
Judge Laurence H. Ginsberg, 105, 120
Julian M. Whitaker, 75, 81, 83
Ketek, 59–62, 59, 60, 61, 62, 108, 134, 135, 137, 144, 145, 146
Legislation
   end prior restraint on claims, 114-117
   mandate due process in Medicare, 118–119
   meaningful judicial review, 109–111
   preventing industry capture, 107–110
   preventing relinquishment of law-making power, 107
   protect public from unsafe drugs, 111–114
   punish officials for violations, 111
Leo Lutwak, 48-49, 51-52
Lester A. Crawford, 43-44
Magna Carta, 12
Medicare, 8, 34, 35, 36, 37, 39, 40, 41, 42, 46, 95, 96, 97, 98, 99, 100, 101, 104, 114, 128, 129, 139, 142, 143, 144
   audit, 98–101
   audit appeals process, 100–101
   Medicare Audits, 98-101
   Medicare Appeals, 99-101
   Medicare Part B, 96-101, 118-119
   Medicare Part D, 34, 35, 36, 39, 128, 129, 144
   cost of program, 36–37
   Medicare Prescription Drug Imrovement Act, 34-36
"Mediocre Care," 96
Michael M. Landa, 87
Non-steroidal anti-inflammatory drugs, 66, 86
Montesquieu. *See* Charles de Secondat de Montesquieu
Nutrition Labeling and Education Act, 70
Omega-3 fatty acids, 72, 114
Osteoarthritis, 86
Paxil, 62–65, 62, 63, 136, 144
Pearson litigation, 68-69, 71-79, 81-83
Pharmaceutical industry, 32
   lobbying, 34
   monopoly, 30-32, 47, 69–71, 119
   post governmental employment, 38, 43
Prior restraint, 31-32, 67-69, 89, 114-117
Public choice theory of economics, 29–30, 29
Redux, 48, 108

Regulatory state, 8-9, 24-28, 66
Rent-seeking, 31-32, 39
Rezulin, 49–52, 49, 50, 51, 52, 56, 108, 131, 132, 146
Richard Foster, 37
Robert I. Misbin, 50-52
Ron Paul, 5, 107, 117
Ronald Reagan, 1, 5, 120
  deregulation, 1
  Reaganites, 2, 3–4
Rosemary Johann-Liang, 52
Russell Katz, 63-64
Sam Adams, 15
Sandy Shaw, 71-82
Saw Palmetto, 83
Separation of Powers, 14, 17–20, 102
Steven K. Galson, 54
Structure/function claims defined, 85
Structure/function claims, 85, 88-89, 114-117
Switch in time that saved nine, 25-26
Thomas Gordon, 17
Thomas Jefferson, 10, 11, 15, 16, 17, 68, 123, 124, 126, 143
Thomas A. Scully, 37
Unnaccountable Congress, 21-24
Unsafe drugs, 42, 47-66, 108
Vioxx, 43, 53–59, 53, 54, 55, 57, 58, 66, 108, 135, 145
Whitaker ligitation, 75, 79-85, 86-89, 117
Zoloft, 62–65, 62, 63

ABOUT THE AUTHOR

Jonathan W. Emord is a constitutional and administrative law attorney who has litigated before the federal courts and agencies for the past twenty-three years. He has defeated the Food and Drug Administration a remarkable six times in federal court. He served as an attorney in the Federal Communications Commission during the administration of President Ronald Reagan and as a Vice President of the Cato Institute. He is the author of two other books, *Freedom, Technology, and the First Amendment* (1991) and *The Ultimate Price* (2007). He is the host of the weekly Health, Law, and Politics radio program on the Talk Star Radio Network.

PRAISE FOR THE RISE OF TYRANNY

"Jonathan Emord's many legal victories over the federal bureaucracy have made him a hero of the health freedom revolution. I am pleased to recommend Mr. Emord's *Rise of Tyranny* to anyone concerned about restoring constitutional government."
- Ron Paul, U.S. Congressman

"*The Rise of Tyranny* is a beacon of truth. Throughout history the world has depended on a precious few to win and preserve our great civil rights. Jonathan Emord is one of those precious few. His book explains the tyranny of federal agencies and proposes a plan that we can implement to restore our liberties. This book will truly make a difference for hundreds of millions of Americans."
- Charles B. Simone, M.D., Oncologist and Immunologist, Simone Protective Cancer Institute

"The Rise of Tyranny is an astonishing achievement. Emord has exposed the very foundations of the tyranny of the FDA and laid bare the corporate-sponsored plot to keep American consumers ignorant, diseased and bankrupt. And yet, beyond the gloom, Emord delivers a realistic formula for reclaiming true freedom in America today. The Rise of Tyranny earns my enthusiastic endorsement. I consider it a must-read book for anyone who wishes to escape consumer enslavement and reclaim their Constitutional liberties in the face of a criminally-operated government."
- Mike Adams, Founder, NaturalNews.com

Purchase additional copies of this book from SentinelPressShop.com